# Stubborn

## *Debra Sue*

JEFFERY TRACEY SR.

PAGE PUBLISHING, INC.
New York, NY

First originally published by Page Publishing, Inc. 2019

ISBN 978-1-64584-163-0 (Paperback)
ISBN 978-1-64584-276-7 (Hardcover)
ISBN 978-1-64584-164-7 (Digital)

Printed in the United States of America

# *Dedication*

IN LOVING MEMORY OF Gwen and James Chapman.

To my wife, Debra Tracey. You are my love, you are my soul mate, and you are my hero.

To my children, Carrie and Eric Nelson and Jeffery Jr. and Lan Tracey. You are awesome children and make me proud.

To my brother-in-law and sister-in-law, John and Terry Sabo. Your generosity and willingness to help others is commendable.

To my sister-in-law, Pamela. Your work in law enforcement helps to keep our communities safe.

To my grandchildren, Charles, Steven, Tyler, Chase, Myla, and Kayla. You are the future. You all make me proud, and I love each and every one of you.

To my great-grandchildren, Evelyn and Sawyer. The future is yours.

# Contents

# *Acknowledgments*

FIRST AND FOREMOST, I would like to thank Debra Tracey for sharing her childhood stories. Without them, this book would not have been written.

I would like to thank Simon Goodway for providing the illustration for the book cover and reconstructing several photos so they could be included in the book.

I would like to thank Chase and Kayla Tracey for providing the sketch illustration used in the book.

# Chapter 1

# THE BEGINNING

Pregnant Gwen

IT WAS THE YEAR of 1953, in a small Texas town named Borger. Borger is located in the Texas Panhandle about fifty miles northeast of Amarillo, Texas. The greatest fear the American public had at the time was that the polio virus would strike in their community. It would be two years before the polio vaccine would be made available to the American public.

Gwen was a beautiful five-foot-eight-inch woman with flaming-red hair and sparkling green eyes. She had a special glow about her that only women being pregnant have. Her husband, Sully, was a former marine. He was a six-foot muscular man with sandy-blond hair and piercing blue eyes. Gwen was eight months pregnant and expecting the birth of their second child next month. Gwen and Sully had a boy named James who would be two in six months. Gwen's best friend, Doris was nine months pregnant, and she was ready to give birth any day now. Doris, already had two boys named Tommy and Ricky. Tommy was four years old, and Ricky was the same age as Gwen's son James.

Gwen and Doris did everything together. They were always shopping together, and they often bought the same baby accessories. Both Gwen and Doris were wishing for a girl this time. Doris would always tease Gwen and tell her she was going to have a baby boy. Doris would say, "You're going to have a boy because you're carrying it low, just like you did with James."

Gwen would reply, "I'm going to have a baby girl. You just wait and see."

Doris would laugh and teasingly chant, "You're going to have a boy. You're going to have a boy."

Gwen would retort, "I'm going to have a girl. You're going to have a boy. I'm going to have a girl, and you're going to have a boy," and then they both would laugh like a couple of teenage girls.

Two days later, September 3, 1953, Doris gave birth to a healthy baby boy. Doris named her third son Billy. Gwen just knew she was going to have a baby girl, and Sully and Gwen had already decided to name her Debra Sue. Gwen was right, and on October 28, 1953, she gave birth to a healthy eight-pound-six-ounce baby girl.

Debra Sue took offense when the doctor lightly slapped her on the bottom to make her gasp for air so she would start breathing on her own. Debra Sue gasped for air all right, and then she let out a loud wailing cry that didn't stop until the doctor handed Debra Sue to her mother.

Gwen gently wrapped her arms around her newborn baby, and Debra Sue immediately stopped wailing. The doctor remarked, "She sure has a set of lungs on her," and then instructed the nurse to take the baby to the nursery and clean her up while the mother was also being cleaned.

Gwen reluctantly handed her newborn baby to the nurse. As the nurse gently cradled the baby in her arms, Debra Sue immediately started thrashing her arms and legs, and the wailing began. The strong love bond between mother and daughter occurred instantly and would last forever. Gwen could hear her baby girl wailing as the nurse walked down the hallway to the nursery.

Gwen thought, *Debra Sue sure has a set of lungs on her. I'm going to have my hands full with this baby girl.*

Gwen was right. Debra Sue would prove to be a stubborn little girl. One might even say that Debra Sue would prove to be a stubborn, spoiled child. And one might even go as far as to say Debra Sue would prove to be a stubborn, spoiled rotten child. A child that would have to have it her way or no way.

Debra Sue fussed and cried the entire time the nurse was cleaning her up. After the nurse finished cleaning the baby, she wrapped her up in a soft infant blanket and rocked her back and forth in her arms. Debra Sue continued fussing and crying.

The nurse finally realized that Debra Sue was not going to stop fussing and crying, and she carried her back to Gwen's room and handed Debra Sue to her mother's loving, outstretched arms. She immediately stopped crying. Gwen gave Debra Sue a bunch of kisses on both sides of her fat little cheeks. Then she started nursing Debra Sue, and she soon fell fast asleep on top of her mother's chest.

Three days later, Sully and Gwen took Debra Sue home where she met her brother James for the first time. Gwen cradled Debra Sue in her arms and sat down in a rocking chair and said, "James, come see your sweet baby sister."

James walked over and stared at his baby sister. He gently rubbed the top of his sister's head. Debra Sue grinned at her brother, and a bond was immediately made that would never be broken.

James as Toddler

# CRAWLING TO MOM

DEBRA SUE WAS LYING on the carpet next to Sully's feet. She was content as she chewed on a teething ring while her dad read the sports section in the newspaper.

That was until she saw her mom come walking into the room. Gwen walked past Debra Sue and sat down in the rocking chair on the other side of the room. Debra Sue cooed and grinned at her mom, hoping she would come over, pick her up, and rock her back and forth in the chair.

But Gwen wanted to rest from cleaning the kitchen and ignored Debra Sue. She picked up a book and started reading. Stubborn Debra Sue decided if her mother would not come to her, then she would go to her mother.

While lying on her belly, she put her right forearm in front of her and bent her left leg. Then she pulled with her forearm and pushed with her leg and started scooting toward her mother. She repeated her technique and scooted closer to her mother.

Sully peered over the top of his newspaper and noticed Debra Sue scooting on her belly toward Gwen. Being a former marine, he remarked, "She looks like a wounded soldier crawling to her mother." Gwen looked over her book, smiled with pride, and watched Debra Sue continue to scoot toward her.

Gwen remarked, "She is too young to be trying to crawl. She isn't even six months old yet."

Sully said, "That's my stubborn Debra Sue. She's my little wounded soldier girl," and laughed.

Debra Sue looked up and saw that her mother was watching her. She stopped scooting and cooed and grinned at her mother, hoping she would get out of her rocking chair and come pick her up. But Gwen just went back to reading her book.

Stubborn Debra Sue went back to work, and she started scooting closer to her mother. When she finally arrived at Gwen's feet, she started cooing to get her attention. But Gwen just ignored Debra Sue and kept reading her book. Spoiled, stubborn Debra Sue had enough and wasn't about to let her mother ignore her anymore, and the wailing began.

Gwen put the book down and picked up wailing Debra Sue. She immediately stopped wailing and gave her mother a big grin. Gwen started rocking back and forth and kissed Debra Sue on the cheek and said, "You are getting so spoiled."

Debra Sue soon fell fast asleep, cuddled in her mother's arms, with a sly smile on her face.

One day, Debra Sue was scooting toward her mother, when she realized that scooting on her belly was taking way too much time to get to her mother.

She figured there had to be a quicker way. She put both her hands in front of her and raised her face and chest up. Then she pulled both her knees under her. Debra Sue was now on her hands and knees and started rocking back and forth. Stubborn Debra Sue couldn't figure out why she wasn't moving closer to her mother. She rocked back and forth harder, and yet she still didn't move an inch.

Debra Sue moved both hands forward at the same time and fell face first onto the carpet. Stubborn Debra Sue didn't let that stop her. She got back on her hands and knees and started rocking. This time, she moved one hand forward, then her knee, then her other hand forward and then her other knee.

Debra Sue moved forward, closer toward her mother. This would work. She repeated her new technique and crawled closer to her mother. Before Debra Sue knew it, she was at the feet of her mother. After all that exertion, Debra Sue expected her mother to be pleased and would pick her up immediately. But Gwen was reading a book and ignored her daughter. Debra Sue was not going to put up with that and started crying. Gwen ignored her crying and continued reading her book.

Debra Sue became frustrated that her mother was not picking her up, and she began banging her forehead against the floor for attention. Gwen thought, *She is just going to have to quit being so spoiled,* and kept on reading.

But stubborn Debra Sue was not going to let her mother ignore her, and she just kept banging her forehead against the floor until it started to get black and blue. Gwen gave in and bent over and picked up her daughter and said, "You are getting spoiled rotten," as she sat back down in her chair

Debra Sue gave her mother a big grin as she snuggled into her arms. Stubborn Debra Sue had figured out how to crawl. By crawling, she could get to her mother much quicker, and at six months old, Debra Sue was crawling all over the place.

This was the first sign of Debra Sue demonstrating that where there is a will, there is a way.

Chapter 3

# SPOILED ROTTEN

DEBRA SUE WAS CRAWLING all over the place, and sometimes she would get rug burns on her knees. But that didn't stop stubborn Debra Sue from crawling. She would crawl over to her brother James to play with him and sometimes just to pester him. But most of the time, she would crawl to her mother. She rarely crawled to her father.

One day, Sully was sitting on the couch, and Gwen was sitting in the corner on the easy chair. Debra Sue was crawling toward her mother. As she crawled by her father, Sully outstretched his arms and coaxingly said, "Come to Daddy."

Debra Sue had her sights set on her mother, and she wasn't going to let anything deter her from her path. She continued crawling past her father.

Sully again coaxingly said, "Come to Daddy, sweetie."

Stubborn Debra Sue ignored her father and kept crawling to her mother. With his feelings hurt, Sully blurted out, "Oh, I guess I have to treat you like shit like your mother does, huh! So you will want to come to me."

Gwen was shocked and said, "That was a horrible and ugly thing to say to your daughter."

Sully grunted, stood up, and stormed out of the room. Debra Sue ignored her father, and when she reached her mother, Debra Sue said, "Mama."

Gwen smiled and said, "Yeah, you come to Mama," and she bent over and picked Debra Sue up. Debra Sue gave her mother a big grin.

Gwen loved the fact that Debra Sue was her little girl, and she didn't mind her getting under her feet while she was cleaning or cooking.

One day, when Gwen finished waxing the coffee table, Debra Sue pulled herself up on the coffee table and held onto it putting her handprints all over the clean waxed table.

Gwen sternly said, "No, Debra Sue, get your hands off the coffee table."

Startled, Debra Sue plumped down on her butt and said, "No."

Gwen took her dust rag and polished the table for the second time, removing all of Debra Sue's handprints. That didn't stop Stubborn Debra Sue. She must have been proud of seeing her handprints all over the table, because as soon as Gwen finished polishing the table, Debra Sue pulled herself up on the table again and slapped her handprints back onto the table.

Gwen raised her voice and yelled, "I said, No! Get off the coffee table!"

Stubborn Debra Sue was again startled and plumped down hard on her butt and defiantly said, "No!"

Before Gwen wiped off the handprints for the third time, Gwen picked up Debra Sue and carried her to her bedroom and put her in her crib for a nap.

The next milestone for Debra Sue was when she was nine months old. That was when she took her first step and then plumped down on her butt. Debra Sue grabbed a hold of her favorite coffee table, pulled herself up, and took two more steps before plumping down on her butt. Stubborn Debra Sue crawled back to the coffee table, pulled herself up, and took five steps before landing again on her butt. Stubborn Debra Sue refused to crawl back to the coffee table to pull herself up, and she stood up wobbly on her own and walked the rest of the way to her mother. Sully remarked, "It must be taking her too long to get to her momma by crawling, so she figured out how to walk so she could get to her momma quicker."

Gwen was beaming with pride and said, "That's my baby girl. Come to Momma."

Once that first step was taken, it wasn't long before Debra Sue was walking all over the place. By the time she was eleven months old, she was running all over the place. She would chase her brother James, and he would chase his little sister.

One Sunday, Sully was relaxing in his easy chair, sipping on a cup of coffee, and reading his newspaper. Debra Sue was standing next to Sully, watching her brother James riding his wooden rocking horse. As soon as he climbed off the rocking horse, stubborn Debra Sue ran over and climbed on the horse. She raised her fist in defiance and rode the rocking horse wildly, grinning from ear to ear.

Debra on rocking horse

Sully heard the commotion and peered over the top of his newspaper. He grinned with pride and said, "That's my tough little soldier girl," and returned to reading the sports section.

They were awesome siblings and loved to play with each other. But when Gwen came into view, Debra Sue would run to her mother and grab a hold of her leg. Sometimes she would almost trip Gwen when she bumped into her. Debra Sue would be under foot so often, Gwen had difficulty getting her household chores completed.

Wednesday was laundry day, and as usual, Debra Sue was under foot. After lunch, Gwen said, "Children, it's time to take your nap."

James said, "Yes, ma'am." And headed toward his room. Gwen followed James with Debra Sue at her heels.

Gwen pulled the covers on top of James and kissed him gently on the forehead and said, "I love you, James."

James replied, "I love you, Momma."

Gwen bent down and picked up Debra Sue and carried her to her bedroom. As Gwen tucked the covers over Debra Sue, Debra Sue said quite clearly, "Luv, Mama."

Gwen gasped and could not believe her ears. A tear of joy slid down her cheek as she said, "I love you, darling."

Gwen left Debra Sue's bedroom, leaving the door wide open like she always did. Back in those days, they didn't have baby monitors to listen to their babies as they slept in their rooms. Gwen picked up a laundry basket full of dirty clothes and carried it down the hallway to the garage.

Gwen was so thankful that Sully had just purchased a washing machine for her. She used to have to go to the neighborhood washeteria. Gwen would have to take Debra Sue and James with her or leave them with a babysitter.

Now all she needed was a dryer. But she didn't mind hanging the clothes on the clothesline in the backyard. The clothes always had a fresh clean smell on them when they were dried on the clothesline.

Gwen placed the dirty clothes into the washing machine. After the washing machine started, Gwen walked up the hallway toward the living room. She glanced into her daughter's and son's bedroom as she passed. Both children were sleeping soundly.

She smiled as she thought, *All is perfect. Life is wonderful.* Gwen sat down in the rocking chair and picked up her book and began reading. After about thirty minutes, she put the book down and headed down the hallway to the garage. The shoes clacking on the hardwood floor awakened Debra Sue as Gwen walked past her bedroom. Debra Sue caught a glimpse of her mother and started crying to be picked up. Gwen ignored Debra Sue and continued to the garage. Spoiled Debra Sue was not about to have her mother ignore her, and the wailing began.

Gwen thought, *She has only been asleep for thirty minutes. I will let her cry herself back to sleep.*

Gwen took the clothes out of the washing machine and put them in the clothes basket. The entire time, stubborn Debra Sue continued to wail, and with each passing minute, she wailed louder and louder. It finally woke up her brother James.

*So much for Debra Sue crying herself back to sleep,* Gwen thought.

Gwen stuffed the last of the wet clothes into the basket and then walked briskly up the hall to Debra Sue's bedroom. James climbed out of bed and peeked into the hallway to see what the fuss was all about. Gwen saw him peeking and sternly said, "Get back in bed right now, James! You have thirty more minutes of nap time!"

James said, "Yes, ma'am," and climbed back into bed and slipped under the covers.

Gwen walked into Debra Sue's room where she was standing up, shaking back and forth on the crib's bars. The wailing immediately stopped as Debra Sue watched her mother approach her and started clapping her hands, just knowing that she would be picked up and cuddled in her arms.

That didn't happen. Gwen picked her up all right and laid her right back down on her back and covered her up and said, "You go back to sleep, young lady. You have thirty more minutes of nap time." Debra Sue said, "Luv, Mama," hoping that would be enough for her mother to pick her back up.

But Gwen just turned around and walked out. Oh, no, stubborn, spoiled Debra Sue was not going to put up with that, and the wailing began. Gwen ignored her wailing. She went to the garage and picked up the basket of wet clothes and took them outside to hang up on the clothesline. As she was hanging up the clothes on the clothesline, she could hear her stubborn Debra Sue wailing.

The wailing did not stop until Gwen finally returned to her crib and picked her up. As soon as Gwen picked her up, the wailing stopped and a sly smile appeared on Debra Sue's face.

Gwen cradled her little girl and remarked, "You are getting so spoiled."

Every time Debra Sue would see her mother walk past her bedroom doorway, stubborn Debra Sue would start wailing. If Gwen did not come in and pick her up, the wailing would get louder, and stubborn Debra Sue would bang her forehead against the crib rails until Gwen picked her up.

It got to the point where Gwen would get down on her hands and knees and crawl past Debra Sue's bedroom door so she would not see her.

When Gwen told her best friend Doris that she would have to get down on her hands and knees to crawl past Debra Sue's bedroom door, Doris remarked, "You are spoiling that girl. You need to let her cry herself back to sleep."

Gwen said, "I've tried that. But Debra Sue is so stubborn, that if I don't pick her up, she will start banging her forehead against the crib until her forehead is black and blue."

Doris replied, "It sounds like Debra Sue is already spoiled rotten. You're going to have your hands full with that girl."

Gwen said, "I think you are right." But that would not matter, because the bond between mother and daughter was immense and would last forever.

Gwen holding Debra

# Chapter 4

## THE POLIO VIRUS SCARE

GWEN'S BEST FRIEND DORIS and her husband, Nick, decided to celebrate Tommy's birthday at a State Park. They invited Gwen and Sully
to bring the family and celebrate Tommy's birthday with them. Now
Gwen had always let James play outside in the dirt and in the mud,
and she never gave it a second thought. After all, James was a boy.

But when it came to Debra Sue, Gwen was overly protective.
She wanted Debra Sue to be the cleanest, healthiest, and most beautiful little girl there was.

Gwen never let Debra Sue play in the dirt and mud. Whenever
Debra Sue did get slightly dirty, Gwen would immediately wash her
thoroughly. She didn't want her little girl catching any germs or diseases.

Therefore, Gwen was reluctant to take Debra Sue to the State
Park where all those mosquitoes, insects, and bugs lived. But Debra
Sue was so energetic and running all over the place, that she allowed
Sully to talk her into accepting the invitation. Sully had said, "The
kids will have a blast, and maybe it will get rid of some of all that
energy Debra Sue has."

Both families had a wonderful time celebrating Tommy's birthday. Both parents laughed as the children played tag, dodging in and
out of the trees. Debra Sue could run fast enough to catch James,
Ricky, and Billy. But she couldn't catch the eldest boy, Tommy. Both
parents allowed the children to play until the sun dropped below the
top of the tree line. Then they packed everything into their cars and
headed home.

A few days later, Debra Sue was being ornery and was laughing as she dangled a worm in her outstretched hand while chasing her brother.

James was screaming, "Stop it, Debra! Stop it! I'm going to tell Mom on you!"

Debra Sue laughed all the harder and kept chasing him. She was just about to catch him when she stumbled and fell. Debra Sue had always been very agile and had been running around wild and free for about four months now. She had never stumbled and fallen down.

The next day, Debra Sue saw her mom in the kitchen. As she ran over to Gwen, her left foot dragged just a little, and she tripped on the rug in the kitchen and fell. Her head narrowly missed the edge of the cabinet.

Gwen quickly ran to Debra Sue and picked her up, checking her all over. Gwen asked, "Are you okay, sweetie?"

Debra Sue rubbed her knee, smiled, and said, "Okay, Mama."

Gwen gave a bunch of kisses on both of Debra Sue's fat little cheeks. Debra Sue stayed next to her mom, occasionally bumping into her, as she closely watched her mother making some corn bread for tonight's supper.

At the supper table, Gwen looked at Sully and remarked, "I've been noticing Debra Sue stumbling and falling more often. Do you think we should take her to the doctor?"

Sully replied, "She's a toddler. Kids are always clumsy and falling down at that age. I wouldn't worry."

As the days passed, Debra Sue continued to stumble and fall down more often. Gwen noticed she wasn't running around and chasing her brother James like she loved to do. Instead she was sitting on the floor next to her as she was cooking dinner. That evening at supper, Gwen said, "Doris told me that Tommy and Billy are in the hospital at Amarillo. They both came down with polio. Tommy is so ill he had to be placed into a lung machine. She said Billy's polio wasn't as serious. I think they may have caught the polio virus at the park. Since we were with them, I'm concerned Debra Sue might have caught the polio virus since she is starting to stumble more often."

Sully refused to believe his little girl had polio and sharply said, "Debra Sue doesn't have polio! She is a toddler, and it's normal for her to stumble and fall!"

Sully and Gwen retired to the living room to relax and read the newspaper. The newspaper was always having headlines about someone coming down with polio. There were headlines about how the new and improved polio vaccine would soon be available for the American public. The newspaper stated that Amarillo opened a polio clinic for the Texas Panhandle area. People were coming from as far away as Oklahoma and Borger, Texas.

Gwen remarked, "They opened a polio clinic in Amarillo. That's why Doris took Tommy and Billy to Amarillo."

Sully said, "Debra Sue does not have polio. You worry too much."

The next morning, Gwen visited Doris, and they went together to the hospital where Tommy and Billy had been admitted. When Gwen arrived back at her home, she immediately picked up Debra Sue and cuddled her in her arms. Gwen couldn't shake the feeling that Debra Sue was stumbling and falling down more often and might have polio.

That evening, Debra Sue followed behind her mom as usual when they retired to the living room after supper. Debra Sue usually kept up with her mom and would occasionally bump into her as they walked. But tonight, Debra Sue was walking slower than usual and fell behind. Gwen was already sitting in her rocking chair by the time Debra Sue walked into the living room.

Debra Sue stumbled on the carpet and fell. Instead of getting up and walking, she started crawling toward her mother. Gwen was concerned when she noticed Debra Sue crawling toward her instead of getting up and walking.

Gwen said, "I'm worried Debra Sue might have polio. I think we need to take her to the doctor in Amarillo."

Sully put down his paper. He was still refusing to believe his daughter might have polio and roughly said, "Debra Sue does not have polio! She is only a toddler, and she is going to fall down from time to time! It's getting late, and she is probably just tired! That's why she is crawling!"

That night, when Gwen tucked Debra Sue in bed, Debra Sue started coughing. Gwen felt her forehead and said, "You feel warm. I'm going to take your temperature, sweetie." Then Gwen bent over and gave Debra Sue several kisses on both sides of her fat little cheeks. Gwen went to the bathroom and returned with a thermometer. Gwen was right. Debra Sue had a 103-degree fever. Gwen tucked the covers around Debra Sue and said, "I'm going to take you to the doctor tomorrow."

The next morning at breakfast, Gwen said, "I'm taking Debra Sue to the doctor to have her checked out."

Sully worked at a petroleum plant and said, "Be sure to take her to the company doctor so our insurance will pay for the doctor bill."

After breakfast, Sully picked up his lunch bucket and thermos and kissed Gwen on the forehead and reminded her, "Be sure to take her to the company doctor."

Gwen reassuringly said, "I will."

James asked, "Mommy, what is a company doctor?"

Gwen replied, "He is a doctor that will take real good care of your sister."

Debra Sue asked, "Get doll?"

Gwen laughed and said, "No. But I will buy you a doll after the doctor sees you, sweetie." Gwen dropped James with a neighbor, and then she took Debra Sue to Sully's company doctor.

Gwen explained to the doctor, "Debra Sue has always been very agile and has been running around since she was nine months old. Lately, I've noticed Debra Sue has been stumbling and falling down more often. She even went back to crawling the other day. She also has been more tired than usual. We were at a park about a month ago with my friend's children, and they came down with polio. I'm afraid Debra Sue might have caught the polio virus."

The doctor examined her thoroughly, checking her ears, mouth, and throat. He placed the stethoscope on her chest and had Debra Sue breathe deeply. After he examined her, he said, "She just has a cold causing her to cough and to be fatigued. Make sure she drinks plenty of fluids, especially orange juice, and that she gets plenty of rest for the next few days. She will be fine."

Gwen was relieved that Debra Sue didn't have the polio virus and said, "Thank you, Doctor. I'll make sure she drinks plenty of fluids and gets plenty of rest."

Gwen was driving home when Debra Sue looked at her with a big grin and asked, "Get doll?"

Gwen was going to drive straight home and put Debra Sue to bed so she could rest but decided spoiled Debra Sue would be so disappointed if she didn't get her doll. So Gwen drove to the Woolworth's store instead. Gwen and Debra Sue were walking hand in hand when they entered the store. Debra Sue's left foot dragged just a little, and she tripped over the mat just inside the door. If it wasn't for her mom holding her hand, Debra Sue would have fallen to her knees. Gwen asked, "You okay, sweetie?"

Debra Sue replied, "Okay, Mama."

They walked to the doll section in the store, and Debra Sue picked out a beautiful doll and squealed with delight, "This doll, Mama!"

Gwen said, "Okay, sweetie. Now let's pay for the doll and go home."

Gwen picked up James from the neighbor. Then she put Debra Sue in bed and tucked her new doll next to her and said, "You take a nap and rest so you can get better." Usually, Debra Sue would fuss when it was time to take a nap. But it had been a busy day, and Debra Sue went to sleep with a big grin on her face as she hugged her cuddly new doll.

At supper, Sully asked, "Did you go to the company doctor?"

Gwen replied, "Yes. The doctor said Debra Sue has a cold, and that is why she is always tired and stumbling."

Pleased with himself for being right, Sully said, "I told you, she didn't have polio."

Gwen remembered Debra Sue stumbling when walking into the Woolworth store and said, "I sure hope that company doctor is right, and Debra Sue doesn't have polio."

Sully reassured Gwen, "Debra Sue doesn't have polio. Stop your worrying."

A week passed, and Debra Sue was still sluggish. In fact, she seemed to be stumbling more and more often. Gwen was growing more and more concerned about her daughter. It was wash day, and Gwen put Debra Sue and James down for their naps as usual.

Only today, when it was time to get the clothes out of the washing machine to hang on the clothesline, Gwen did not get down on her hands and knees to crawl past Debra Sue's doorway. Instead Gwen let her shoes clack a little harder on the hardwood floor as she walked past her bedroom.

Secretly Gwen was hoping to see her spoiled Debra Sue standing in her crib and start to wail when she walked past her. She wouldn't even be upset if stubborn, spoiled Debra Sue banged her forehead against the crib just because she didn't pick her up.

But that didn't happen. Debra Sue was sleeping soundly. As Gwen put the damp clothes into the basket, she couldn't get the fact out of her head that Debra Sue was falling more and more often.

Gwen exited the back door in the garage and hung up all the damp clothes on the clothesline in the backyard. She walked back into the garage and then into the hallway. Gwen let her shoes clack loudly on the hardwood floor as she returned to the living room. She peeked into Debra Sue's bedroom. She was still sleeping. All of a sudden, Gwen became weary from worry, and she sat down in her rocking chair to rest.

The next morning, Gwen walked into Debra Sue's bedroom to get her dressed. Debra Sue usually would be standing in her crib just waiting for her mother to pick her up. But not this morning. Gwen was a little surprised that her stubborn Debra Sue wasn't standing in her crib, shaking the rails, and waiting impatiently for her mother to pick her up. Gwen looked into the crib and noticed Debra Sue's left leg was crumpled under her back in a distorted way. She knew immediately something was terribly wrong. Gwen picked Debra Sue up out of the crib, and Debra Sue's left leg just flopped down and dangled.

Tears started streaming down Gwen's face as she carried her little girl out the bedroom. Debra Sue's left leg was flopping back and forth like there were no muscles at all in the leg.

Gwen screamed, "Sully, get up and get dressed right now!" Debra Sue startled from her mom's screaming and started to cry. Debra Sue's left leg was flopping back and forth with each step her mom took.

Gwen realized she had to calm down and reassure her little girl and said, "It's all right, sweetie. Everything is going to be okay."

Sully jumped out of bed and asked, "What's going on?"

Gwen yelled, "Look at her left leg! It has no muscle control! We're going to take her to the hospital in Dallas right now!"

Sully yelled, "No! We'll take her to the Amarillo hospital! It is much closer!"

Gwen was not about to take her little girl to Amarillo and defiantly yelled, "No! We're not taking Debra Sue to Amarillo! That is where Tommy passed away from his polio. I will not take Debra Sue to that hospital. We are going to the hospital in Dallas."

James was getting scared from all the commotion and asked, "Why does Debra have to go to the hospital, Daddy?"

Sully trying to reassure his son said, "We're going on a little road trip. Won't that be fun?"

James replied, "Okay."

Debra Sue stopped crying and whimpered, "Okay."

Gwen said, "Sully, go get James dressed, and I'll get Debra Sue dressed, and then we'll drive to Dallas, okay?"

Sully replied, "Okay. Calm down now. Everything is going to be okay."

They drove straight through to Dallas, Texas. It was a tiresome six-hour drive when they finally pulled up in front of the emergency room at a children's hospital. The ER doctor took one look at Debra Sue's left leg and stated they would be admitting her into the hospital for further tests.

Debra Sue was eighteen months old when the doctor told Gwen she had polio in both legs. Gwen broke down and cried as she sat on the bed next to Debra Sue.

The doctor tried to reassure Sully and Gwen and said, "It is a good thing you brought her into the hospital when you did. If you had waited any longer, the polio virus would have continued to attack her on the left side and up into her left arm. This could have caused paralysis in her left arm. We will have to perform a biopsy on both legs to determine the extent of the damage the polio virus caused. The polio virus that attacked her right leg appears to be minimal, and with rehabilitation, she should be able to maintain the majority of her muscles in that leg. After the biopsy, we will fit her for two leg braces and start training her to walk with the assistance of crutches. She will have to stay in the hospital for about three weeks."

Gwen broke down and started to cry. Seeing her mother crying scared Debra Sue, and she started crying also. Gwen wiped her tears from her eyes and said, "You're going to be just fine, sweetie," and then gave Debra Sue a big hug and gave her a bunch of kisses on both sides of her fat little cheeks.

Debra Sue said, "Luv, Mama."

The doctor admitted Debra Sue into the hospital. By the time the nurse wheeled Debra Sue into her room, it was dark outside. The room was a ward and had a row of six beds. It had a big window that ran from the ceiling to the floor that overlooked the street below.

The nurse put Debra Sue in the third bed by the big window. After Gwen tucked the covers in nice and snug over Debra Sue's little body, Gwen stood up and said, "Sweetie, we have to leave now."

Debra Sue got wide-eyed with fear. She raised up her outstretched arms to her mother for her to pick her up and said, "Mama, Mama."

Gwen fought back the tears and said, "The nurses will be at your side. If you need anything, call for a nurse."

Stubborn Debra Sue pooched out her bottom lip pouting and stammered, "I'm...I'm scared, Mama."

Gwen wiped the tears from her cheeks and said, "I'll see you soon, honey," and leaned over and gave Debra Sue a bunch of kisses on both of her fat little cheeks.

Sully leaned over and gave Debra Sue a big hug and said, "You be a tough soldier girl, okay?"

Debra Sue didn't know what a tough soldier girl was, but she said, "Okay," anyway.

Sully and Gwen waved goodbye from the doorway and left the room. There were no children in the beds on either side of Debra Sue, and she felt all alone.

Debra Sue looked out the big window and saw several car's taillights as they were driving slowly down the street. Debra Sue was in a trance in watching all the car's taillights driving down the street.

She picked out one of the car's taillights and thought, *I bet Mama is in that car. I wish I was in that car with them. I'm scared being here all alone.* It became too much for little Debra Sue to bear, and she began to cry. She cried herself to sleep.

Even though the next three weeks were very busy for Debra Sue, she missed her mother and cried herself to sleep almost every night. After the biopsy was performed on her legs, Debra Sue started her physical therapy.

Debra Sue was fitted for two leg braces and given two crutches. The doctors were amazed at how quickly Debra Sue adapted to the leg braces and crutches. One doctor commented, "She is so tiny. That is one tough little girl. I have never seen anyone this young walk that quickly with leg braces and crutches."

Within three days, Debra Sue was walking with her leg braces and crutches without any assistance. Occasionally, her crutches would hit a slick spot on the floor, and she would tumble down. It was difficult for her to stand up without being able to bend her knees.

Stubborn Debra Sue would pull herself up on a chair, or a bed or any other piece of furniture she could find. When there weren't any fixtures to pull herself up on, she figured out how to use her crutches to pull herself up to a standing position.

Stubborn Debra Sue was not about to let anything stop her from getting up and walking again. With the aid of those little crutches, she was able to steady her gait. Before long, she was a pro at walking in her leg braces and crutches.

A week later, the doctors were ready to release Debra Sue from the hospital. Sully and Gwen walked into the hospital ward. Gwen was carrying a bag and smiled at her little girl and said, "I got something for you, sweetie," and gave Debra Sue a big hug and kissed both sides of her fat little cheeks.

Debra Sue was grinning from ear to ear as she said, "Luv, Mama."

Debra Sue looked into the bag and pulled out a nice cuddly doll. She gave the doll a big hug. That would be the start of Debra Sue's collection of dolls. One that would last forever.

The nurse looked at Sully and Gwen and said, "You can go check Debra Sue out of the hospital and pull the car around to the front of the hospital. I will push Debra Sue out to the front of the hospital in a wheelchair."

Sully and Gwen gave Debra Sue a hug and then left to go check her out of the hospital and bring the car around. The nurse and Debra Sue waited out in front of the hospital for about ten minutes when Sully pulled up in front of the hospital.

Gwen exited the car and went over to Debra Sue and picked her up out of the wheelchair and carried her to the car. Both had great big grins on their faces because they were so happy they were going home.

Sully said, "We're out of here," and sped off. The drive home was a long six-hour drive, and they were glad to be finally home.

Sully parked the car in front of their house and said, "Wait a minute. I want to take a picture of Debra Sue walking back home."

Sully ran into the house and retrieved the camera. He started taking pictures as Gwen walked behind Debra Sue while holding onto Debra Sue's outstretched hands. Debra Sue was beaming with pride as she was able to walk up to the house wearing her new leg braces.

Gwen and Debra with leg braces

However, there would now be a new daily ritual for Debra Sue to start the day. Gwen would come into her daughter's room, pick her up, and give her a bunch of little kisses on both sides of her fat little cheeks. Then she would fight back the tears as she strapped Debra Sue's little legs into the cold steel braces.

Debra Sue would gasp and say, "It's cold, Mama."

Gwen would reply, "I'm sorry, sweetie," and finish dressing her. Then she would pick up Debra Sue and hug her and give her a bunch of little kisses on both sides of her cheeks. Debra Sue would giggle and was now ready to start her day.

It wasn't long before Debra Sue was out in the back yard playing tag and chasing after her brother James. Debra Sue would use her crutch to tag James in the back and then twirl around and run away with her little crutches moving ninety to nothing. The whole time she was laughing her head off.

Gwen remarked, "She doesn't let those leg braces and crutches slow her down one bit."

Debra on crutches

Sully said, "Debra Sue is one tough little soldier girl."

The doctor was right about his diagnosis when he said the polio virus had not attacked the right leg as severely as the left. The polio virus had only attacked about 20 percent of the muscles in the right leg. But Debra Sue would have to have physical therapy for quite some time.

Stubborn Debra Sue did her physical therapy religiously. She worked very hard to complete all her leg exercises during her physical therapy sessions. She was so determined to strengthen the muscles in her legs, that she would do her leg exercises before and after her scheduled physical sessions.

Sometimes she would work so hard during the day that her legs would ache for hours at bedtime, and she would cry herself to sleep from the pain. But that would not stop stubborn Debra Sue from doing her leg exercises first thing in the morning.

After a year of painful physical therapy, Debra Sue had strengthened the muscles in her right leg so much that she no longer had to wear a brace on her right leg. Stubborn Debra Sue proved at a very young age that where there is a will, there is a way.

*Chapter 5*

---

# SIXTH BIRTHDAY

---

GWEN WAS EIGHT MONTHS pregnant with their third child when the family moved to Pasadena, Texas. Sully's employer opened a new plant there. He was offered a position, and he accepted.

Because Sully was a former marine, he was able to obtain a VA loan, and they bought a new three-bedroom house. They had a great big yard with a swing set.

James and Debra Sue loved that swing set. They would swing back and forth every day. James would always give Debra Sue a push in the back to get her going. Then he would go sit in his swing, and off they would swing as high as they could.

Gwen just adored at how close James and Debra Sue had grown. Whenever they were swinging on the swings, they were always so happy and laughing.

Debra and James swinging

Debra Sue was always trying to swing higher than her brother. When it was time for them to come into the house, Gwen would have to yell, "Get off the swing! It's time to come into the house!"

James would obediently say, "Okay, Momma," and jump off the swing and come into the house.

Stubborn Debra Sue would keep on swinging until her mother yelled, "If you don't come into the house right now, you won't be swinging on that swing set for a week! Do you understand me, young lady?"

Debra Sue pooched out her bottom lip and started pouting, as she stopped swinging and then walked slowly to the house grumbling under her breath with each step.

A month later, on October 16, 1956, Gwen gave birth to her third child. She was a healthy baby girl, and they named her Terry. A year later, Gwen gave birth to another baby girl. And then another year later, Gwen gave birth to their last baby girl, and they named her Pamela.

Debra Sue now had an older brother and three younger sisters. She always tried to help her mother with the chores. Debra Sue never let her handicap get in the way with her helping her mother.

Debra Sue quickly made friends with all the children in the neighborhood. As the years passed, and Debra Sue became older, she was having sleepovers with the girls who lived next door. They loved playing with all of Debra Sue's dolls. They would sit in a circle on the floor and dress up their dolls in all the latest fashions.

Debra Sue especially loved to put on the latest fashionable shoes on her dolls. She would imagine herself wearing pretty fashionable shoes on both her feet.

Debra Sue had to wear army-style laced shoes that covered her ankles. The left shoe had to be attached to her leg brace. Debra Sue hated the ugly brown clodhopper shoes. They looked like boy's shoes instead of girl's shoes.

Debra Sue's brace was nothing pretty to look at either. The brace started at the bottom of her left foot, and it ran to the top of her left thigh, stopping just below her left hip. The brace had ugly thick brown straps up and down. Ugly thick brown straps wrapped around her ankle, her shinbone, her knee, and finally around her thigh.

Stubborn Debra Sue hated her ugly brace, and she was always trying to hide it. She would wear long dresses or baggy pants so they would cover her brace. When she sat down on the floor or on the ground, she would position herself so the brace would not be seen by her friends. She always wanted to look like all the other kids whenever possible.

When it was time for Debra Sue's sixth birthday, Gwen invited all of Debra Sue's friends over to celebrate it with her. There was a house full of boys and girls celebrating her sixth birthday. Debra Sue was grinning from ear to ear as she was opening her presents.

The wrapping on one present was giving Debra Sue a hard time as she tried to remove it. Stubborn Debra Sue pooched out her bottom lip and ripped it off. When she saw what it was, she held it up over her head with a big wide grin on her face and showed it to all her friends. It was a plastic dinnerware and tea set. It was her favorite gift.

Debra birthday plates

Now Debra Sue and her friends could pretend to have dinner and tea with her dolls. Since she had started kindergarten, one of her gifts was a blackboard and chalk to draw on. Debra Sue was always very inquisitive and very smart. She loved to learn and try new things.

After all the presents were opened, Gwen brought in the birthday cake. Instead of it being one large birthday cake, Gwen had made six individual cupcakes and placed one candle on each cupcake. Then everyone sang "Happy Birthday" to the birthday girl. Debra Sue puckered up her lips and blew out all the candles on the cupcakes.

Debra birthday cake. Illustrated by Simon Goodway.

This was Debra Sue's day, and it was a great day. That was until her sister Terry tried to butt in. Debra Sue and her girlfriends went into her bedroom to play house with her new dinnerware and tea set. Terry followed behind her girlfriends into Debra Sue's bedroom.

Debra Sue got upset when Terry tried to butt in and play with her friends. Debra Sue pushed her sister away and sternly said, "Go play in your own room! This is my birthday!" But Terry was stubborn and refused to leave Debra Sue's bedroom.

This irritated Debra Sue, and she yelled, "Terry, you just want to be the center of attention! Go play in your own bedroom!"

Terry did a little dance to show off and then sat down on the floor and picked up a doll and started playing with it.

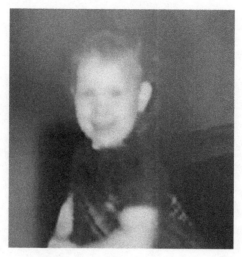

Terry

Stubborn Debra Sue gave her sister a big frown and then yelled, "Mom! Terry is bothering us! Terry won't go to her room and let me play with my friends! This is my birthday, not Terry's birthday! Make her go to her room!"

Gwen hollered, "Terry, go to your room and let Debra Sue play with her friends!"

Debra Sue smirked and said, "Ha, ha."

Terry stuck her tongue out at Debra Sue and reluctantly left the bedroom. Debra Sue picked up her doll and handed it to her friend sitting next to her and asked, "How do you like her outfit? Don't she have beautiful shoes?"

Her friend replied, "Yes," and picked up a doll and started brushing the doll's hair.

This was Debra Sue's day, and she had a wonderful time celebrating with all her friends. Debra Sue was now six years old.

James at party

# Chapter 6

---

# FIRST GRADE

---

WHEN DEBRA SUE'S GIRLFRIENDS started the first grade, she wanted to go with them. Debra Sue asked her mother, "Why can't I go to the first grade with my friends?"

Gwen replied, "You're not old enough yet."

Debra Sue said, "I'm six years old just like they are."

Gwen explained, "The law says a child has to be at least six years old when the school year starts in September, and since your birthday is in October, you will have to wait another year before you can go to the first grade."

Stubborn Debra Sue pouted and said, "That's not fair. I will be seven years old when I'm in the first grade, and everyone else will be six."

Gwen said, "I'm sorry, sweetie, but that's the way it is." The year passed slowly for Debra Sue. But she made new friends, and finally, September rolled around, and Debra Sue would be going to the first grade. Gwen was ready to take Debra Sue shopping for new clothes. Gwen hollered, "Debra Sue, get dressed! We're going shopping for school clothes!"

Debra Sue sadly asked, "Mom, can they attach a pretty shoe onto my brace instead of this ugly old shoe? All my girlfriends wear nice pretty shoes, and I have to wear this stupid ugly ankle shoe that looks like a boy's shoe. Why can't the shoemaker attach a girl's dress shoe onto the brace?"

Gwen was sad that her daughter had to wear a boyish-looking ankle shoe on her left foot and said, "I'll see if the shoemaker can attach a pretty dress shoe to your brace. But until then, you will have to wear the shoe that is attached to the brace. It's really not that ugly."

Stubborn Debra Sue said, "If it's not really that ugly, then you wear it and see how you like it."

Gwen said, "Go get into the car."

Stubborn Debra Sue pooched out her bottom lip and pouted as she walked to the car.

At the department store, Debra Sue was happy and grinning from ear to ear as her mom picked out several pretty new dresses. One of the outfits was a poodle skirt. It would turn out to be Debra Sue's favorite skirt. Even the fifth graders would be giving her compliments on her poodle skirt.

As they passed the shoe department, Debra Sue ran over and picked up a pretty pair of white dress shoes and squealed with delight, "I love these shoes, Mom."

Gwen said, "Try them on, and if they fit, we'll get them. I will see if the shoemaker can attach the left shoe to your brace."

The next day Gwen and Debra Sue went to the shoemaker. Gwen handed the white dress shoes to the shoemaker and asked, "Can you attach this shoe to Debra Sue's leg brace?"

The shoemaker pointed to the shelf on the wall where there were two pair of brown ankle shoes and two pair of black ankle shoes and replied, "These are the only shoes that I have to attach to the brace."

Gwen said, "They all look like boys work shoes. You can't get any girl shoes to attach to the brace?"

The shoemaker replied, "It's a shame they don't make pretty shoes to attach to braces. But these are all the shoes that I have to work with."

Disappointed, Debra Sue pooched out her bottom lip and pouted as she left the store still wearing her ugly ankle shoe on her leg brace. She thought, *I hate you ugly shoe. I feel like burning you to ashes.*

At the house, Gwen said, "Debra Sue, go take off your brace, and I will put white shoe polish on your shoe to make it look prettier."

Debra Sue minded her mother and took off her leg brace. She could walk around without her leg brace if she placed her hand on her knee to lock her knee in place. But occasionally, she would forget to place her hand on her knee and her leg would buckle and down she would fall, skinning her knees.

Gwen did her best to dye the shoe with white shoe polish to make it match her right dress shoe. But the shoe just looked like a dirty brownish-white ankle shoe. Gwen felt sad and disappointed that she couldn't make the shoe look pretty like the right shoe. She dyed the shoe two more times with the white shoe polish. In the end, it still looked like a dirty white ankle shoe.

Debra Sue was going to start the first grade wearing her new pretty dress that her mom had bought her. That morning, Debra Sue paraded around in her bedroom wearing her new outfit. She loved her pretty white dress with blue flowers, but she hated her ugly shoe on her left foot.

She thought, *This is going to be so embarrassing to wear this ugly shoe to school. I'm going to tell Mom I'm sick and stay home.*

Just then, Gwen hollered from the kitchen, "It's time to go to school!"

Debra Sue walked into the kitchen and said, "I'm sick, Mom."

Gwen felt her forehead and said, "You don't have a fever. You're just nervous. I'll take you to school for your first day."

Gwen drove Debra Sue to school and parked the car and said, "Okay, are you ready for me to walk you to your classroom on your first day of school?"

Debra Sue looked out the car window and saw several children walking past the car toward the school building. She bent over and said, "I have to tie the shoelace on my ugly shoe."

The shoelace wasn't really untied. Stubborn Debra Sue was just acting like she was tying her shoelace until all the children had past her by and were walking into the school building.

When Debra Sue saw the last child walking into the building, she said, "Okay, Mom. I got my shoelace tied nice and tight so I won't fall."

Stubborn Debra Sue would continue this maneuver every day because she did not want the other school children gawking at her leg brace when she was walking into the building.

Gwen knew what Debra Sue was doing and was very patient and allowed her to go through the motion of tying her shoe until all the students were inside the school.

Gwen exited the driver side and walked around the car and opened the car door for Debra Sue. Gwen started escorting Debra Sue to her classroom on her first day of school. Gwen would continue this tradition, and escort Debra Sue to her classroom on the first day of school for the next six years.

Debra Sue finally put a stop to it when she noticed Gwen was the only mother who escorted her child into the classroom in the sixth grade. Stubborn Debra Sue would refuse to let her mother escort her to her classroom in the seventh grade.

But today, on Debra Sue's first day of school, Gwen would escort her daughter to her classroom. And today, Debra Sue was glad that her mother was escorting her into her classroom because she was just a little scared.

While they were walking down the hallway toward her classroom, Debra Sue looked down at her feet and thought, *I don't know why they can't attach my pretty shoe to my brace. This is really humiliating having to wear this ugly shoe on my left foot and a pretty dress shoe on my right. This is so embarrassing.*

But when Debra Sue saw all her girlfriends at school, she ignored her brownish-white ugly shoe and ran over to them with a big grin on her face. They immediately started talking girl talk and giggling. Debra Sue was very kind and told her girlfriends how much she loved their new shoes.

Gwen would escort her daughter to her classroom only on the first day of school. After that, she would drop Debra Sue off at the curb and let her walk into the school like all the other students did.

During the second week of school, after Debra Sue was finished tying her shoelace and was walking toward the school, Gwen noticed Debra Sue was limping just a little. It appeared her left leg was a little shorter than the right leg. She decided to make an appointment with the doctor when she returned home.

The next week, Gwen took Debra Sue to the doctor. The doctor examined Debra Sue as she walked up and down the hallway. Then he measured her right leg and then her left leg.

The doctor said, "Due to the polio, Debra Sue's left leg is not growing at the same rate as the right leg. Her left leg is slightly shorter than her right leg. The right leg may continue to grow longer than the left. Debra Sue may have to get a shoe that has a thicker sole for her left foot to even out her gait."

Gwen asked, "Isn't there anything we can do?"

The doctor replied, "There is a great hospital in Houston called the Hospital Clinic for Crippled Children. It is a teaching hospital, and they specialize in children with orthopedic problems. If you are interested, I'll notify the hospital, and someone will schedule an appointment with you for your daughter."

Gwen said, "Yes. If they can help my daughter, then I want to go there."

A month later, Debra Sue had an appointment to meet with the doctors at the Hospital and Clinic for Crippled Children. It was October when Gwen and Debra Sue were going to meet with the new doctors.

Gwen held Debra Sue's hand as they walked into a huge waiting room. There were ten rows of long wooden benches running from one side of the waiting room to the other side.

The reception desk was on the sidewall where everyone had to sign in before taking a seat on the benches. The doctor's office was in the corner of the front side of the waiting room.

There were men and women restrooms on both ends of the waiting room. On the front side of the waiting room, there was a sign above the restroom's doors stating "White Women" and "White Men." On the back side of the waiting room, there was a sign above their restroom's doors stating "Colored Women" and "Colored Men."

Even though it was eight thirty in the morning, the waiting room was crowded. Most of the people were sitting on the benches that were closer to the doctor's office. Gwen went over to the reception desk and signed in for Debra Sue. They found a half-empty bench near the colored women's restroom.

Debra Sue said, "Mom, I have to go to the restroom."

Gwen said, "Okay, I'll stay here and hold our seats."

Debra Sue stood up and started walking toward the colored women's restroom. Gwen quickly walked over to Debra Sue and gently grabbed her arm, turned her around, pointed to the white women's restroom, and said, "Sweetie, you have to use the women's restroom on the front side of the room."

Debra Sue obediently obeyed her mother and started walking toward the white women's restroom. Debra Sue was confused as to why she couldn't use the restroom that was closer to her bench. She didn't understand why she would have to walk all the way to the front side of the room to use the restroom, when one was so close. That just didn't make sense. She would have to ask her mother about that when she returned to her bench.

Debra Sue used the restroom, washed her hands thoroughly, and walked back to her bench. Just as she sat down on her bench, she noticed a very small man walking into the waiting room. Debra Sue thought, *He's not much taller than me.*

Debra Sue couldn't take her eyes off the little midget and kept staring at the man as he walked to the reception office and signed in. She forgot all about asking her mom why she had to use the bathroom at the front of the room, when there was one so close.

After the midget signed in, he sat down on their bench a few feet from Debra Sue. Debra Sue had never seen a midget before and couldn't help but stare at him. She noticed his feet couldn't touch the floor just like her feet couldn't touch the floor when sitting in the bench. Gwen noticed Debra Sue was staring at the midget and quietly said, "Why are you staring at the man sitting across from you?"

Debra Sue said, "That man is so little."

Gwen said, "You see, sweetie. You are just curious, and you started to stare at the man. Your classmates are just curious about your leg brace, and that is why they stare at you. You don't like people staring at you, and that man probably doesn't like you staring at him. You should just look at him, say hi, and politely look away."

Debra Sue said, "I've never thought about it like that, Mom. I won't stare at him anymore."

An intern came into the waiting room and called out Gwen and Debra Sue's names. They followed the intern to the examination room. The doctors explained to Sully and Gwen that the hospital was a training hospital for new intern doctors.

The examining room was a large oval room. Up above, there was a balcony with several rows of stadium-type benches. This allowed the doctors and interns to view the patients down below, as they walked around the oval room.

The doctor told Sully and Gwen that Debra Sue would have to undress and put on bikini-type underwear. Then she would have to walk around the oval room while all the doctors and interns evaluated her gait.

Debra Sue was very shy, and she looked pitifully at her mother and asked, "Do I have to get undressed and walk around in front of all those doctors?"

Gwen replied, "It is all right, sweetie. These doctors need to evaluate you so they can help you walk."

When Sully, Gwen, and Debra Sue reached the examining room, they were shocked to see about twenty children in the examining room. There were both boys and girls standing in line with nothing on but their bikini-type underwear. The doctor instructed Debra Sue to go behind the curtain and disrobe and put on her underwear.

Debra Sue started to sob and stammered, "Do I...I...I have to take off all my clothes, Mommy?"

Tears started to run down Gwen's cheek as she said, "You have to do what the doctors tell you to do. I will be right here with you, sweetie."

Debra Sue went behind the curtain and removed her clothes and put on her bikini-type underwear. The doctor instructed Debra Sue to get in line behind the last child. Stubborn Debra Sue was so shy and embarrassed that she refused to come out from behind the curtain.

The doctor had to go behind the curtain and escort Debra Sue to stand in line behind the last boy. Then he walked over to a pulpit and picked up a microphone. He called out the name of the girl who was standing in front of the line.

The doctor instructed her to walk around the room. The little girl had tears running down her cheeks as she walked around the room. The doctor spoke into the microphone and informed the doctors and interns sitting in the balcony above what the little girl's diagnosis was.

Then the doctor called out the next name and said her diagnosis. They marched the children around the arena like they were cattle. The doctors were indifferent to the children crying from fear and feeling so embarrassed.

Finally, the doctor behind the podium called Debra Sue's name. Debra Sue started crying and looked over to her mother for help. Gwen tried to fight back the tears from streaming down her face but was unsuccessful as she motioned for Debra Sue to walk around the examining room.

Debra Sue started walking around the room. She was thankful they let her wear her leg brace. Otherwise, she just knew she would have tripped and fallen. That would have been really embarrassing. The doctor on the microphone told the observing doctors and interns that Debra Sue had polio.

Debra Sue was so embarrassed that she drowned out the rest of what the doctor was saying on the microphone. She just wanted to be done parading around the arena like she was an animal.

The doctors evaluated Debra Sue thoroughly. They watched her gait as she walked in her brace. Then they evaluated her muscles with the brace off.

The doctors all agreed they could help her. The doctor explained they could transplant muscles from her back to her left leg. If the muscle transplant was successful, Debra Sue may be able to walk without a brace.

Sully and Gwen were excited and hopeful that Debra Sue might be able to walk one day without a brace. They immediately scheduled a date to admit Debra Sue into the Hospital and Clinic for Crippled Children.

On the way home, Gwen said, "Debra Sue, next Monday, you are going to be admitted into the Hospital and Clinic for Children." Gwen thought, *That hospital is so insensitive for calling it a Hospital*

*Clinic for Crippled Children.* Gwen refused to say the word "crippled" when she referenced the name of that hospital. She would always call it the Hospital and Clinic for Children.

Debra Sue didn't know what "admitted into the hospital" meant. She became scared and stuttered, "Wha…wha…what is getting admitted into hospital?"

Gwen realized Debra Sue was getting scared and tried to reassure her, "Everything will be just fine, sweetie. We have to fill out some paperwork so you can stay at the hospital for your surgery. That is what admitting is. The doctors are going to transplant some muscle from your lower back to your leg so you can walk without a brace."

Debra Sue shrieked with delight, "So I can wear pretty shoes to school?"

Gwen laughed and said, "Maybe. We'll see."

That next Monday, Sully and Gwen admitted Debra Sue into the hospital. After the paperwork was completed, a nurse escorted Sully, Gwen, and Debra Sue to the ward where Debra Sue would be staying for her surgery.

The ward was an oblong room with a large window at the end of the room. There were three beds lined up against the left side of the wall, and three beds lined up on the right side of the wall. All three beds on the right side had a child lying in them. On the left side of the wall, there was a child lying in the bed at the far end, near the window. The other two beds on the left side of the room were empty.

The nurse took Debra Sue to the middle bed on the left side of the wall and said, "This will be you bed, sweetie."

Debra Sue looked up at her mother wide-eyed and stuttered, "I…I…I'm scared, Mommy."

Gwen picked Debra Sue up, gave her a big hug, and sat her gently on the bed. Gwen reassuringly said, "You don't have to be scared. The nurses here will take good care of you."

The nurse said in a commanding voice, "Say your goodbyes now. You can see each other during visiting hours from now on."

Debra Sue started to realize her mother would be leaving her all alone and said, "Don't leave me, Mommy. I'm scared," and tears started running down her cheeks.

Gwen was unsuccessful in fighting back her tears and tearfully said, "We have to go now, sweetie. We'll be back at visiting hours, okay?" and gave Debra Sue a bunch of kisses on both sides of her cheeks.

Debra Sue hugged her mother and said, "Okay. I love you, Mommy."

Gwen said, "I love you too, honey."

It would be two days before the doctors would schedule Debra Sue for surgery. The evening before the surgery, two nurses walked into the ward. The first nurse was a tall heavyset woman with a frown on her face.

The second nurse was a smaller woman and had a warm smile. The heavyset woman walked up to Debra Sue's bed and asked, "Are you Debra Sue?"

Debra Sue replied, "Yes, ma'am," and thought to herself, *Who else would I be.*

The nurse with the warm smile said, "We have to prepare you for your surgery tomorrow. Okay, sweetie?"

Debra Sue replied, "Okay."

The tall heavyset nurse placed a mat at the foot of the bed and then intimidatingly said, "Scoot down toward the foot of the bed so we can rub the iodine on your leg."

Debra Sue said in an apologetic voice, "I'm sorry. I didn't know I should scoot down to the foot of the bed."

The tall heavyset nurse irritatingly said, "How else are we going to rub iodine all over your leg without getting it all over the sheets?"

Debra Sue scooted all the way down to the foot of the bed to please the nurse. The nurse with the smiling face said, "Scoot down a little bit more so your entire leg will fit on the mat."

Debra Sue scooted down a little more, and the nurse said, "That is perfect, honey."

The nurses rubbed the iodine all over her left leg from her ankle to her thigh and then on her back. When the nurses finished rubbing iodine on Debra Sue's leg and back, they started to leave the ward.

Debra Sue didn't know what the iodine was for, and she was afraid to move so she asked the nurses, "Can you move me back up to my pillow?"

The tall heavyset nurse sarcastically said, "You're not a baby. You can move yourself back onto your pillow."

The nurse with the warm smile walked back to the bed and said, "Yes, darling. I'll move you back to your pillow." The nurse lifted Debra Sue under her arms and placed her gently back onto her pillow.

Debra Sue said, "Thank you, ma'am," and thought, *She sure is a nice nurse.*

After the nurses left, Debra Sue thought, *I thought what they were doing to my leg was very important, and I shouldn't move it. I feel so stupid and embarrassed for not knowing that I could move my leg. But that heavyset nurse didn't have to be so mean.*

At 6:00 a.m., Gwen walked into the ward carrying a stuffed teddy bear and walked over to Debra Sue's bed and said, "I brought you a gift, sweetie."

Debra Sue squealed with delight and grabbed her teddy bear and hugged it tight and said, "Thank you, Mommy."

At 7:00 a.m., the two nurses who put the iodine on Debra Sue's leg walked into the ward and over to Debra Sue's bed and said, "It's time for us to take you to the operating room."

Debra Sue panicked and stammered tearfully, "Ma...Ma... Mommy, I'm scared."

Gwen leaned over and gave Debra Sue a big hug and said, "It's okay, honey. Everything is going to be just fine." Then Gwen turned her head away and wiped the tears from her eyes.

The nurses pushed Debra Sue's hospital bed out of the ward and down a corridor. They turned left onto a corridor, then turned right onto a corridor, then went down a corridor with a ramp, then walked straight ahead, then up a corridor with a ramp, and finally wheeled the hospital bed into the waiting room. They wheeled the hospital bed for what seemed forever to Debra Sue.

Debra Sue kept looking back to see if her mother was still coming with them. It looked like Gwen was huffing and puffing just to keep up with the nurses. Debra Sue said, "I'm sorry you have to walk all this way, Mommy."

Gwen said, "Don't be silly. This is nothing," and blew Debra Sue a kiss.

When it was time for Debra Sue to go into the operating room, Gwen gave Debra Sue a bunch of kisses on both sides of her cheeks. The nurses had to interrupt Gwen and said, "We have to take her now."

Debra Sue started to cry as the nurses wheeled her away from her mother into the operating room. The nice nurse smiled reassuringly at Debra Sue and held her hand and said, "Everything is going to be okay, darling."

In the operating room, the mean nurse put a mask over Debra Sue's mouth and nose and held it firmly in place. Debra Sue didn't like the smell of the anesthesia medicine and tried to pull the mask from her face. But the mean nurse pressed the mask down hard on her face until Debra Sue fell asleep.

Debra Sue woke up in her hospital room with Gwen gently rubbing her forehead. She had a cast that went from her left foot all the way to her left hip. The cast then wrapped around her lower body and continued up to her chest. Debra Sue remarked, "I look like a mummy."

Sully and Gwen had to chuckle at that remark, and they both said, "Hi, sweetie."

Since Debra Sue was in a body cast, she had to rest at an angle with the head of the bed raised. The bed had a wooden plank on it, and the mattress was put on top of the wooden plank. As the wooden plank became higher toward the head of the bed, it had little slots of open space in the plank.

As the weeks passed, Gwen had to leave the hospital to take care of Debra Sue's brother and sisters. But Gwen never missed a day to visit her sweet Debra Sue during visiting hours. Every time Gwen walked into the ward, she would bring Debra Sue a gift. Gwen never visited Debra Sue without bringing her a gift.

Debra Sue looked forward to her mother coming to visit her, and she didn't care if she brought a gift or not. She just wanted her mother to be by her side. Debra Sue made sure she always said, "Thank you for the gift, Mommy."

When visiting hours were over, Gwen would lean over and give Debra Sue a bunch of kisses on both cheeks and then leave. Debra Sue would place her gifts into the little open slots in the wooden plank. That way, she could play with her gifts and admire them when she was all alone.

One visit, Gwen brought a stuffed monkey holding a banana. The stuffed monkey was too big to fit into the wooden slot in the plank. That was just fine with Debra Sue because she always was hugging and snuggling her stuffed monkey with the yellow banana.

Volunteer workers would come to the hospital every evening with cookies and juice for the children. Debra Sue looked forward to the cookies and juice. The only problem was that after she drank the juice in the evening, she would occasionally wet the bed.

The second time Debra Sue wet the bed, the heavyset mean nurse scolded her and roughly said, "Stop peeing the bed! You're too old to be peeing the bed!"

Debra Sue was humiliated and trying not to cry stammered out, "I'm...I'm...I'm sorry."

The mean nurse angrily said, "Don't be sorry! Just stop peeing the bed!"

Debra Sue thought, *I hate you. You're a mean nurse.*

Two nights later, the volunteer workers came around with cookies and juice. Debra Sue took two cookies and a bottle of juice. She thanked the workers and ate the delicious cookies and washed them down with the juice.

That night, Debra Sue wet the bed. The morning nurse came in and immediately saw the wet bedsheets. In a rage, the nurse snarled, "If you don't stop peeing the bed, I'm going to punish you!"

Debra Sue didn't know the meaning of the word punish, and she became scared of the, hateful nurse. Debra Sue fought back her tears and in a quivering voice said, "I...I...I am so sorry. I won't pee the bed no more. I promise. I'm...I'm...so sorry."

The mean nurse roughly moved Debra Sue from one side of the bed to the other as she changed the bedsheets. When the mean nurse left the room, she muttered under her breath loud enough for Debra Sue to hear, "That's ridiculous! Peeing the bed at that age!"

Debra Sue wanted to yell, "*You're a mean witch! I hate you!*" But just said, "I'm sorry," once again. Debra Sue didn't know how the mean nurse was going to punish her. She knew it must be something really awful.

From Debra Sue's bed, she could see into the hallway when the doors were left open. There was a large opening in the wall that was covered by a metal plate.

Debra Sue had seen workers lift up the metal plate and shove bedsheets and covers into the opening. The bedsheets and covers would disappear into the hole. Then the workers would shut the lid back down. Debra Sue just knew that if she peed the bed one more time, that the mean nurse was going to pick her up and push her into the opening in the wall.

Debra Sue was afraid she would disappear forever and never be able to go home again. She feared for her life and started to cry. After she had cried out all her tears, Stubborn Debra Sue started planning her escape from the hospital.

Debra Sue was going to get away from that mean nurse one way or another. Since Debra Sue was in a body cast, she was unable to get up and walk out of there.

Debra Sue's bed was next to the wall, so she stretched out her arms so her hands could grasp the wall. She tried to scoot the bed along the wall to the door. The bed moved just a little. She was going to make her escape.

A male nurse walked into the room and watched Debra Sue trying to move the bed and asked, "What are you doing?"

Debra Sue didn't tell the male nurse she was trying to escape from the hospital because that heavyset mean nurse was going to punish her. Instead she lied and said, "I'm bored and tired of being locked up in this room all the time."

The male nurse said, "I don't blame you. I'll see what we can fix up for you so you can get out of your room from time to time." The male nurse left the room. Debra Sue tried to move the bed again, but it was too heavy, and she grew tired and gave up trying to escape. At least for today.

About twenty minutes later, the nurse returned with a low flat four-wheel wooden dolly. He placed a mat and a pillow on the dolly and said, "Okay. I'm going to lay you on your belly on top of the dolly. Then you can use your hands on the floor to move the dolly to wherever you want to go. How does that sound?"

Debra Sue replied, "That sounds like fun."

The male nurse lay Debra Sue facing downward on top of the dolly. Debra Sue immediately took off propelling herself with her hands on the floor. She headed out the door and down the hospital hallway. The male nurse was caught off guard at how quickly Debra Sue moved on the dolly and had to trot after her. He hollered, "Slow down, Debra Sue! Let me catch up with you!"

Debra Sue just laughed and kept scooting down the hallway. She was enjoying her new freedom. The male nurse allowed Debra Sue to scoot around for about ten minutes and then instructed her to scoot back to her room.

He didn't want her to over exert herself. Stubborn Debra Sue pooched out her bottom lip and pouted, as she scooted herself back to her room.

Debra Sue spent her seventh birthday in the hospital. It was evening, when Gwen walked into the ward carrying a birthday cake with seven candles. A nurse entered the ward rolling a cart with a pitcher full of juice and paper cups. Gwen, the doctors, and the nurses sang "Happy Birthday" to Debra Sue.

When they finished singing "Happy Birthday," Gwen lit the seven scattered candles and said, "Okay, sweetie. Make a wish and blow out the candles."

Debra Sue paused a minute to make a wish. Then she thought, *I wish Mommy would take me home with her tonight.*

Debra Sue took a deep breath and blew hard on all the burning candles. Debra Sue was ecstatic when she blew out all the burning candles. She just knew her wish would come true.

Then Gwen handed Debra Sue her present. Debra Sue squealed with delight after she ripped off the wrapping paper on her present. Gwen had given her a gorgeous curly-haired blond baby doll. It even came with a brush so Debra Sue could brush her curly hair. It was her most favorite present of all times. Debra Sue gave her mother a big hug and said, "Thank you, Mommy. I love you."

Everyone ate the birthday cake and drank the juice and had a wonderful time. Everyone except for Debra Sue. It was getting late, and Debra Sue was so afraid that she might wet the bed if she drank anything. She was so afraid that she refused to eat any cake because she thought it might make her thirsty.

When Gwen was getting ready to leave for the night, Gwen asked, "Is everything okay, sweetie? I noticed you didn't eat any cake or drink anything."

Debra Sue asked, "What does punishment mean?"

Gwen inquired, "Why do you ask that?"

Debra Sue replied, "A mean nurse yelled at me for peeing the bed, and she said she was going to punish me if I pee the bed one more time."

Gwen became furious and asked, "What nurse said she was going to punish you?"

Debra Sue replied, "The heavyset day nurse."

Gwen stormed out of the room and started yelling at the nurses sitting at the nurse's station. Gwen was livid and yelled, "Don't you ever tell my daughter you will punish her!"

Then she stormed to the doctor's office. When she returned to the ward, she looked at Debra Sue and said, "No one will ever be punishing you, sweetie. You don't have to worry about that anymore."

Debra Sue gave her mom a big hug and said, "I love you, Mommy. I blew out all the candles on my birthday cake so my wish would come true. I wished that you would take me home with you tonight. Are you going to take me home with you?"

Gwen fought back her tears and said, "Sweetie, you just told me what you wished for. If you want your wish to come true, you can't tell anyone what you wished for. I would take you home with me tonight, but the doctors want to be able to watch over you until you are all healed. It's for your own good that you stay in the hospital."

Debra Sue pooched out her bottom lip and pouted as she gave her mother one last hug before her mother left the hospital ward.

One good thing did come out of Debra Sue's experience with the tall, heavyset mean nurse though. Debra Sue never wet the bed again. Debra Sue was in her second month of being in the hospital.

She would scoot down to a room where all the children would gather for school. The hospital provided a teacher to teach the children so they wouldn't fall behind in their grades. Debra Sue studied hard and made all As.

The hospital was always doing something for the children. One afternoon, the male nurse, who made Debra Sue's dolly, came into the room and said, "The Big Circus is in town. Tomorrow the hospital is going to take all the children to the circus. The hospital has several vans to take the children in wheelchairs. Would you like to go?"

Debra Sue replied, "I can't sit in a wheelchair."

The nurse said, "If you want to go to the circus, we will figure something out so you can go."

Debra Sue squealed with delight, "I want to go to the circus! I've never been to a circus before!"

The nurse said, "Well, okay then. I'll make sure you go to the circus tomorrow."

When Gwen walked into the ward, she didn't even have time to give Debra Sue the gift she was carrying before Debra Sue excitedly screamed, "Mommy, I'm going to the circus tomorrow!"

Gwen said, "Sweetie, you have to wait until they take the cast off before you can travel anywhere."

Debra Sue said, "The male nurse said he would figure something out, and that if I wanted to go to the circus, he would make sure I would go."

Gwen gave Debra Sue several kisses on both her cheeks and then gently rubbed Debra Sue's forehead and said, "Don't be too upset if you can't go to the circus. It is nice the nurse is trying, though."

Stubborn Debra Sue pooched out her bottom lip and pouted before saying, "I'm going to go to the circus."

When it was time for Gwen to leave, she gave Debra Sue a warm hug and kissed her on the forehead and said, "I'll see you tomorrow."

Debra Sue said, "If I'm still at the circus, be sure to wait until I get back. Okay, Mommy?"

Gwen loved Debra Sue's positive attitude and replied, "I sure will, sweetie."

Debra Sue was so excited about going to the circus for the first time. She hardly slept a wink that night. In the morning at 10:00 a.m., the male nurse came into Debra Sue's room pushing a stretcher.

He said, "I told you, we would figure something out. I am going to place the wooden plank on the stretcher and then the mattress on top of the wooden plank. We are going to take you to the circus in an ambulance. Are you ready to go, Debra Sue?"

Debra Sue screamed with delight, "I sure am! But what am I going to do with my toys I have stuffed in the plank?"

The nurse said, "Take them out of the slots and leave them on your bed. You can put them back in the wooden slots when we get back from the circus."

Debra Sue grinned and said, "Okay."

The nurse picked up Debra Sue from her bed and placed her temporarily on the dolly. He took the mattress off the wooden plank that was on Debra Sue's hospital bed and leaned it against the stretcher. He picked up the wooden plank and placed it on top of the stretcher.

Then the nurse took all of Debra Sue's toys out of the wooden slots and placed them on top of the hospital bed. He picked up the mattress and placed it on top of the wooden plank. Finally, the nurse picked up Debra Sue off the dolly and placed her on the stretcher.

Debra Sue asked, "Can I take my pillow for my head?"

The nurse replied, "You sure can," and grabbed her pillow off her hospital bed and placed it gently under her head and asked, "Are you ready to go to the circus?"

Debra Sue thought, *That male nurse sure is kind to go to all this trouble just so I can go to the circus.*

Debra Sue was grinning from ear to ear as she replied, "Yes, sir, and thank you very much for doing this for me."

The male nurse said, "No problem, sweetie. It's my pleasure."

The nurse wheeled the stretcher out of her room, down the hallway, and out the exit doors. He wheeled Debra Sue down a ramp to an ambulance parked alongside several vans. There were several children in wheelchairs being loaded into the vans.

The nurse opened the back doors of the ambulance and loaded Debra Sue into it. The nurse shut the back doors and climbed into the driver's seat. He turned his head around to look at Debra Sue and said, "Are you ready to go to the circus, Debra Sue?"

Debra Sue replied, "Yes, sir."

The nurse said, "Then we're off."

The ride in the ambulance was a bumpy one, and it took about twenty minutes to get to the circus. The nurse parked the ambulance, exited the vehicle, and opened the back doors. He looked at Debra Sue and asked, "Are you okay, sweetie?"

It was a rough ride, and Debra Sue had been bounced around on that hard stretcher. She was very uncomfortable in her body cast, and her body was starting to ache.

Debra Sue put on a big fake grin and said, "I'm doing great."

Debra Sue had a way with making people think she was feeling great even though she would be feeling miserable and be in a lot of pain. Stubborn Debra Sue didn't want anyone feeling sorry for her.

The nurse said, "I'm glad you're feeling great. I thought the ride might have been a little rough for you."

Debra Sue lied and said, "The ride was fun. It's great to be out of the hospital."

The nurse remarked, "That's good. You're going to have a great time at the circus."

The nurse pushed Debra Sue's stretcher to the front row and parked it next to the row of children sitting in wheelchairs. He locked the wheels on the stretcher and sat in a seat behind it.

A bunch of clowns walked toward the children to say, "Hi," to them. Debra Sue was propped up so she could watch the clowns talking to the children in the wheelchairs. They were making animal characters out of balloons and giving them to the children.

One really tall skinny clown with huge ugly yellow shoes walked over to Debra Sue and asked, "What is wrong with you, little girl?"

Stubborn Debra Sue thought, *How rude. Nothing is wrong with me. What is wrong with you?* Debra Sue was feeling miserable and was in pain from the rough ambulance ride as she thought, *I'm not about to explain to you that I got polio when I was little and the doctors operated on my leg.*

Debra Sue sharply said, "None of your business!"

The tall skinny clown with his huge ugly yellow shoes quickly stomped away.

Debra Sue was uncomfortable lying on her back on that hard stretcher, and that tall skinny clown had upset her so much she didn't enjoy the circus. Even though Debra Sue loved dogs, she didn't even break a smile as the dogs jumped through their hoops and did their flips. She did wish she could take the dogs home with her, though.

Debra Sue was in pain and was glad when the circus was finally over, and it was time to go back to the hospital. The nurse wheeled Debra Sue's stretcher back to the ambulance. He loaded Debra Sue into the ambulance and shut the back doors. He climbed into the driver's seat and turned his head around and asked, "Did you have a good time at the circus, Debra Sue?"

Debra Sue again put on a big fake grin and lied, "I had a great time. Thanks for taking me to the circus."

The nurse smiled with self-satisfaction that he was able to make a little girl so happy and said, "You are so welcome."

He never did realize how much pain Debra Sue was in. When they arrived at the hospital, the nurse wheeled Debra Sue's stretcher to the recreation room. There were more circus clowns visiting with the handicapped children that were unable to go to the circus. The clowns were making animal balloons and handing them out along with toys to the children.

The ride back to the hospital seemed to be even more bumpy, and Debra Sue was in a lot of pain and was exhausted, and she asked the nurse, "Could you take me to my room, please?"

The nurse asked, "You're not having a good time?"

Debra Sue tried to give him a weak fake grin and replied, "Yes, sir. But I'm not feeling well, and I'm tired."

The nurse said, "Yes, sweetie. I'll take you to your room. It has been a long day."

The nurse wheeled Debra Sue into her hospital room. Debra Sue grabbed a hold of her pillow as the nurse picked her off the hard stretcher and placed her onto the dolly. The male nurse had to do everything that he did before they left. Only in reverse.

When Debra Sue was finally back in her hospital bed, she said, "Thank you, sir, for taking me to the circus. I had a great time." The nurse said, "You're quite welcome, sweetie. Would you like me to put your toys back into the wooden slots?"

Debra Sue replied, "That's okay. I know what slot each toy goes into. Thank you, though."

The nurse probably never realized how uncomfortable it was for Debra Sue to be at the circus because stubborn Debra Sue was not one to complain.

A female nurse came into the ward and pulled the curtain around Debra Sue's bed, and then she gave her a sponge bath. The nurse then gave Debra Sue some medication, and she was soon fast asleep. It had been an exhausting day at the circus.

Debra Sue was soon dreaming about all the puppy dogs performing their tricks. She dreamt she snuck a puppy dog home with her and even snorted in her sleep.

During the third month of being in the hospital, Debra Sue's leg and back started itching under the cast.

Debra Sue would look pitifully at her mother and say, "My back is itching so bad. Please get something and scratch my back."

Gwen picked up a clothes hanger and straightened it out. She took the hanger and slid it down inside the cast and moved it up and down.

Debra Sue would sigh, "Oh, that feels so good, Mommy. Keep doing it. Will you scratch my leg now?"

Gwen pulled out the clothes hanger from inside the cast on her back and inserted it into the leg cast at her foot and started scratching. Finally, it was time for the body cast to be removed and the physical therapy to begin. When the cast came off, Gwen was horrified that she had been scratching her back and leg where the wounds were. She realized she could have caused an infection with that dirty clothes hanger.

After being in the hospital for over six months, and all the physical therapy was completed, it was time for the doctors to give a final evaluation to see if the operation was a success.

Unfortunately, the operation was not successful. The muscle transplant did not take, and the operation had failed. The polio virus had destroyed the neurons in the muscle nerve endings.

There were four weeks left in the school year when Debra Sue was released from the hospital. Debra Sue would have to continue wearing a full leg brace and that ugly shoe to school. Gwen dropped off Debra Sue at school on her first day back.

Gwen said, "I love you, sweetie. Have a great day."

Debra Sue replied, "I love you, Mommy."

Stubborn Debra Sue bent over like she was tying the lace on her ugly clodhopper shoe until all the school children entered the school. Then, Debra Sue exited the car, waved goodbye to her mother, and walked toward the school. As she was walking, she looked down at her feet and thought, *All the girls are wearing pretty shoes. I wish I had some pretty shoes instead of this dumb old clodhopper.*

School year was about to end, and it was time for the year-end tests. Stubborn Debra Sue stayed up late several nights in a row, studying hard for all of the tests, and she made As on all her final tests.

So she was very upset when she found out that she had failed the first grade. Debra Sue was crying when she handed the report card to her mother.

She choked out, "I made As on all my final tests, and my teacher still failed me. I won't be able to go to the second grade with all my girlfriends."

Gwen looked at the report card and became angry and yelled, "She can't fail you! I'm going to have a serious talk with her!"

Debra Sue said, "Thank you, Mom."

Gwen went to the school with Debra Sue's report card clenched in her hand. She argued with the teacher for failing her daughter.

The teacher explained, "Half of the grades are based on classroom participation. Since your daughter was not here to participate in the classroom, I had no choice but to fail her."

Gwen yelled, "Debra Sue was schooled in the hospital! The hospital had a teacher that taught class for all the children in the hospital!"

The teacher said, "I had no choice but to fail her. You can take it up with the principal if you like."

Gwen stormed out of the classroom and walked into the principal's office. She yelled at the principal, "Your first-grade teacher failed my daughter because she was in the hospital for half of the school year and did not participate in the classroom! How can she do that?"

The principal explained, "Classroom participation is a vital part of our education, and I'm supporting the teacher's decision to fail your daughter."

Gwen stormed out of the principal's office making one last comment, "This school sucks!" When Gwen drove up the driveway, Stubborn Debra Sue was hopping on her right foot and then on her left foot, playing hopscotch on the sidewalk. Gwen thought, *No wonder Debra Sue is always breaking the straps on her leg brace.*

Gwen exited the car and called out, "Debra Sue, come over here."

Debra Sue stopped hopping and walked over to her mother and said, "Can I go to the second grade with my friends?"

Gwen sadly replied, "No, honey. You have to repeat the first grade. But you will meet new friends."

Stubborn Debra Sue pooched out her bottom lip and pouted as she said, "That's not fair. I'm not stupid. I shouldn't have to repeat the first grade again."

Gwen said, "I'm sorry, honey. But there's nothing I can do."

In September, with no fault of her own, Debra Sue had to repeat the first grade.

# THE FRUIT STAND

DEBRA SUE WAS EIGHT years old when her father went on strike against the petroleum company. The strike lasted for several months, and Sully and Gwen were forced to sell their home. They moved to a poorer neighborhood in Pasadena, Texas.

They rented a cheap two-bedroom home, and Debra Sue now had to share a bedroom with her brother and three sisters. She didn't mind sharing her room.

Ever since James had that convulsion, the doctors had diagnosed him with having a learning disability known as intellectual disability (ID). Debra Sue took it upon herself to be his guardian, and she would watch over him and protect him.

There was a nine-year-old boy who lived across the street, and he was a bully. Debra Sue loved to play hopscotch on the sidewalk. Whenever this bully would see Debra Sue playing outside, he would go over and trip her, causing her to fall down. Then he would laugh, thinking it was funny to see a girl wearing a leg brace fall down.

Stubborn Debra Sue would get up like nothing ever happened and keep on playing. Even though she would often skin her right knee when she fell down. The left knee was protected because it was covered by a heavy-duty strap that was wrapped around the brace.

One Saturday, Debra Sue was looking out the living room window and saw three girls jumping rope. Two of the girls were holding the rope at each end and twirling it around in a big looping fashion. The third girl was in the middle and was jumping over the rope as it passed underneath her.

Debra Sue thought, *I'm going to learn how to jump rope.*

Debra Sue hollered, "James, come here! We are going to jump rope!"

James asked, "We're going to jump rope?"

Debra Sue replied, "Yep. Follow me."

Debra Sue went into the garage and picked up a rope with James following behind her. She took one end of the rope and tied it to the front bumper of the car that was parked in the driveway.

Debra Sue handed the other end of the rope to James and said, "Hold the end of the rope and go stand over there," and she pointed to a spot about five feet from the car.

James went over to the spot where Debra Sue pointed to and stood still like a totem pole.

Debra Sue said, "Start swinging the rope around in a circle."

James said, "Okay, Debra."

Debra Sue walked halfway between where James was standing and where the rope was tied to the car bumper and said, "Okay, James. Start swinging the rope in a circle. But not too fast."

James started swinging the rope in a looping circle. Debra Sue stretched out her arms and raised them up when the rope was looping up and raised them down when the rope was looping down. She did this several times and then took a deep breath and stepped into the path of the jump rope as it was looping upward.

When the rope was looping downward toward Debra Sue's feet, she jumped up. The heavy leg brace kept her from jumping high enough to clear the rope, and it tripped her causing her to fall down and skin her right knee.

James hollered, "You okay, Debra! I'm sorry."

Stubborn Debra Sue ignored the pain, and the blood oozing from her skinned knee. She stood up and said, "I'm fine. James. Let's do it again. This time don't swing the rope so high off of the ground."

James said, "Okay."

Debra Sue got into position, and James started swinging the rope around in a circle. Again, Debra Sue raised her arms when the rope was looping upward and lowered her arms when the rope was looping downward.

When she had the timing down just right, Debra Sue took a deep breath, stepped into the path of the jump rope as it looped upward. This time when the jump rope was looping downward toward her feet, Debra Sue jumped higher, and she cleared the rope. She landed hard, but that didn't bother stubborn Debra Sue. When the rope looped downward again, she jumped high again and cleared the rope easily. Again, she landed hard on her brace.

Stubborn Debra Sue ignored the pain, and she was grinning from ear to ear because she was jumping rope. After she felt confident that she would not fall down and look like an idiot, Debra Sue ran over to the girls next door and jumped rope with them.

They all became very close friends. Debra Sue was always jumping rope with her girlfriends. It was no wonder Gwen had to constantly replace the broken straps on Debra Sue's leg brace.

One evening, Debra Sue wanted to jump rope, but her girlfriends were out of town. Debra Sue hollered, "James, come and hold the jump rope for me!"

James did not respond.

Debra Sue picked up the jump rope and tied it securely to the bumper and hollered louder, "James, come hold the jump rope for me!" James did not answer. Debra Sue knew James loved to play at the neighborhood park. The park was only one block away from their house. The family had their Easter egg hunt there two days ago.

Gwen and James at park.

Debra Sue thought, *James loves to eat. He's probably going to see if he can find some more Easter eggs and candy.* So she headed toward the park.

As Debra Sue arrived at the park, she saw James looking terrified at the top of the slide. Then she saw three boys taunting him and making fun of James. One of the boys was the bully who lived across the street from her.

The bully wanted to look tough in front of his two friends, so he bent down, picked up a rock, and threw it at James. The rock narrowly missed James' head. Even though Debra Sue was wearing her leg brace, she ran toward the bully with remarkable speed and shoved him hard on his chest knocking him backward. He lost his balance and landed on his butt.

Debra Sue yelled, "You leave my brother alone!"

The bully couldn't believe this little girl could knock him down and stammered, "Uh…uh…okay…okay!"

He scrambled up and ran out of the park with his two friends following close behind him. They wanted nothing to do with that little firecracker girl.

Debra Sue walked to the bottom of the slide and asked, "Are you okay, James?"

James replied, "I'm okay. They were bad boys."

Debra Sue agreed, "They sure are bad boys. I'm not going to let them hurt you, brother. I'll protect you."

James said, "I love you."

Debra Sue said, "I love you too. Now sit down and hold on to the side of the slide with both hands and then slide down to me. I'll catch you."

James said, "Okay," and minded his little sister and slid down to her.

Debra Sue spaced her feet apart, leaned forward, and braced herself to catch her brother. He slid into his sister's open arms, and she stopped him at the end of the slide.

From that day on, James would always trust his sister, and that bond would never be broken. Debra Sue helped her brother up from the slide, and they walked hand in hand back toward the house.

At the edge of the park, they saw their mother. Gwen had come looking for James and Debra Sue, and she witnessed her little girl protecting her older brother.

Gwen thought, *Debra Sue is such a tough little girl protecting her big brother. Since Debra Sue gets out of school before James, I'm going to have her walk James home from school every day.*

Since James had a learning disability, he was placed in a school that accommodated special-needs students. It just happened to be the same elementary school that Debra Sue went to. The school was a block and a half away from their home. However, the school was on the other side of a busy road named Red Bluff Road.

In the morning, Gwen would take Debra Sue's three younger sisters to the babysitter. Then she would drop off James and Debra Sue at the elementary school. Debra Sue was in the second grade and got out of school and hour earlier than James did.

As soon as Debra Sue got out of school, she would walk home to drop off her schoolbooks on the kitchen table. Debra Sue did this so her hands would be free to hold her brother's hand when she escorted him home from school. Back in those days, there were no such thing as backpacks.

Carrying the books in both arms made it more difficult for Debra Sue to walk in her leg brace. Since she walked slower while carrying her schoolbooks, she had to make sure there were no cars coming up or down Red Bluff Road before she started to cross over.

Sometimes she would have to wait five minutes before it was safe to cross. Then she would walk as quickly as her heavy leg brace would let her go. After Debra Sue placed her schoolbooks on the kitchen table, she would return to school and wait for her brother.

There was a man operating a fruit stand across from the school. Every time Debra Sue walked past him, the man would always smile at Debra Sue and say, "You be very careful crossing that busy street."

Debra Sue would reply, "Yes, sir."

One day, when Debra Sue was passing the fruit stand to pick up James, instead of the man saying, "Be very careful when you cross the street," he asked, "Would you watch over my fruit stand so I can get something to eat?"

Debra Sue hesitantly looked at the man and said, "I have to get my brother at school so I can walk him home."

The owner said, "I'll only be gone for five minutes, and I'll be right back."

Debra Sue never argued with grown-ups and said, "Okay. I guess."

The owner took off and left Debra Sue watching over his fruit stand. Debra Sue stood guard over his fruit stand and prayed that nobody would stop by. Debra Sue kept looking toward the school across the street to make sure James hadn't come out of the building. She didn't want her brother to be scared standing all by himself waiting for his sister.

Debra Sue was just about ready to leave the fruit stand when the man returned empty-handed. Debra Sue asked, "Where's your food?"

The man said, "I really just had to use the restroom. Thank you for watching my fruit stand. You can pick out anything that you want."

Debra Sue had been eyeing the strawberries and asked, "Can I have the strawberries?"

The owner said, "You sure can," and handed Debra Sue a pint of strawberries.

Then the owner said, "You are such a big girl for watching my fruit stand. Thank you so much."

Debra Sue replied, "You're welcome, sir."

Debra Sue smiled as she walked away clenching the pint of strawberries. She waited until it was clear to cross Red Bluff Road and walked quickly to the school.

She sat down on the bench in the covered waiting area. Debra Sue only had to wait a couple of minutes when James walked out. Debra Sue shared her strawberries with James.

James loved to eat and said, "Thank you, Debra. I love you."

Debra Sue said, "I love you, James." She held her brother's hand and looked both ways making sure there were no cars in sight, and then they crossed the street. As they walked past the fruit stand, the owner again thanked Debra Sue for watching his fruit stand.

Debra Sue smiled and said, "You're welcome."

Debra Sue was pleased as she thought, *The fruit stand owner didn't look at me like I was handicapped. He treated me like a person, and he thought I was capable to watch his fruit stand all by myself.*

Chapter 8

---

# THE MEAN GRANDMOTHER

DEBRA SUE'S GRANDMOTHER LIVED on a farm in Oklahoma. When Sully and Gwen would go on vacation, they would often visit Debra Sue's grandmother in Oklahoma. On this vacation, the grandmother was having a family reunion, and everyone was coming to visit.

Debra Sue was playing outside with her brother, sisters, and all her cousins. They were having a great time playing outdoors. They were chasing the chickens over by the chicken coop. A rabbit came hopping up by the side of the chicken coop.

Debra Sue ran up to Gwen and asked, "Mom, can I take the rabbit home with me?"

Gwen looked at Debra Sue's grandmother and asked, "Is it all right for Debra Sue to take the rabbit home with us?"

Grandmother replied, "If she can catch the rabbit, then she can take it home with her."

Gwen was relieved because she knew there was no way Debra Sue would be able to catch the rabbit and said, "If you can catch the rabbit, then you can take it home."

Debra Sue screamed with delight and took off chasing the rabbit. After chasing the rabbit for about ten minutes, she realized she wasn't going to be able to catch the rabbit. She pooched out her bottom lip and pouted as she walked back to the house without her prize rabbit. Gwen said, "I'm sorry you couldn't catch the rabbit, sweetie."

Debra Sue went over and started talking with her cousins. One of the cousins started bragging about getting five dollars every

Christmas from her grandmother. Another cousin said, "So big deal. I get five dollars every Christmas too."

Debra Sue thought, *I wonder why my grandmother doesn't send me five dollars on Christmas.*

Gwen walked up to Debra Sue and said, "Sully and I are going to go to the store. You make sure your brother and sisters mind your grandmother until we get back."

Debra Sue said, "Okay."

Sully and Gwen left the children with their grandmother, and they went to the supermarket to pick up some groceries for the picnic. The grandmother had invited some of her friends to come over.

The grandmother was ashamed of James and Debra Sue because of their handicaps. Before her friends arrived, the grandmother took James and Debra Sue to a backroom down the hallway.

The grandmother glared at James and Debra Sue and said, "Don't you dare come out of this room until I let you out!" She slammed the door behind her. All the other children were allowed to run around throughout the house and in the yard.

When Sully and Gwen arrived back at the farm, several kids were running around in the front yard playing. Gwen walked up to the front porch where Terry and her grandmother were talking. Gwen looked all around for James and Debra Sue. When she couldn't find them out in the yard, she asked the grandmother, "Where's James and Debra Sue?"

The grandmother said, "Oh. They're in the backroom down the hallway."

Gwen walked down the hallway and hollered, "Debra Sue, James! Where are you?"

Debra Sue yelled, "We're in here!"

Gwen walked to the room where she heard Debra Sue calling from and opened the door. She asked, "Why are you in this room for? Why aren't you and James playing with the other kids?"

Debra Sue replied, "Grandma yelled at us and said we had to stay in this room and not to come out until she let us out."

Gwen was livid and said, "You two go outside and play with the other kids, right now."

James and Debra Sue followed their mother up the hallway. Gwen told Sully what the grandmother did.

Sully became enraged and stormed over to the grandmother, and in front of her friends, he yelled, "Don't you ever lock up James and Debra Sue in a room again! Don't you ever tell James and Debra Sue they can't come out and play with the other kids! If you ever do that again, we will never see you again!"

The grandmother stammered, "I'm…I'm so sorry! I didn't mean any harm!"

Sully and Gwen were so upset, that they packed up the family and left for home. On the way home, Debra Sue asked, "Mom, why did Grandmother make me and James stay in the empty room when everyone else could play outside?"

Gwen said, "Forgive my French. But your grandmother is a bitch."

Debra Sue kept quiet the rest of the ride home. The next morning at breakfast, Debra Sue said, "Mom, my cousins said they get five dollars every Christmas from my grandmother. Why don't I get five dollars from her?"

Gwen didn't want Debra Sue to think her grandmother didn't love her and replied, "She sends you five dollars at Christmas. It just gets lost in the mail because she lives so far away and in another state."

That Christmas, there was an envelope under the Christmas tree addressed to Debra Sue from Grandmother. Debra Sue was delighted when she opened the envelope, and there was five-dollar bill in it. Her grandmother did love her.

However, the next Christmas, there was no envelope under the Christmas tree. Debra Sue realized that her mother must have placed the envelope with the five-dollar bill under the tree and not her grandmother. Debra Sue thought, *I love my mother. And Mom is right, my grandmother is a mean old witch.*

## STRAY ANIMALS

THE HOUSE NEXT DOOR had been abandoned six months ago. The house had deteriorated and was an eyesore for the neighbors. Gwen had instructed James and Debra Sue not to play anywhere near the vacant home.

One day, stubborn Debra Sue was outside playing in her backyard. A cold front had blown through the area, and Debra Sue had on her jacket and mittens. While playing, she heard faint meows coming from the vacant house next door.

Now Debra Sue knew she wasn't allowed to go over to the vacant house. But Debra Sue knew there were some kittens that needed rescuing from that vacant house.

So stubborn Debra Sue walked to the back of the house and noticed the kitchen window was broken. She could tell the meow sound was coming from inside the house.

Debra Sue found a rusty bucket on the ground and placed it upside down under the kitchen window. She stood on the bucket and pulled herself up onto the window sill and scooted inside.

As she landed on the sink, her right leg scrapped against a shard of glass that was lodged inside the window frame. Debra Sue ignored the pain from the cut in her leg and scrambled up and started walking inside the home. She kept listening to where the meows were coming from. The house was filthy, and spider webs were everywhere.

Stubborn Debra Sue did not let the spider webs deter her. She finally found the little kittens in the back bedroom in a closet. There were five little kittens, and all of the kittens were very thin and mangy looking.

They looked adorable to Debra Sue. She took off her jacket and laid it on the filthy floor. She picked up the five mangy kittens and placed them on her jacket and then wrapped them up in it.

Debra Sue carried the kittens to the kitchen window and peered out. She was afraid she would hurt the kittens if she dropped them to the ground. So she picked up her bundle of kittens, walked to the back door, unlocked it, and exited the vacant house. Debra Sue made sure she shut the back door tightly and took the kittens to her house.

Debra Sue laid the kittens wrapped in her jacket onto her bed. Then she went and found an empty box in the garage. On the way back to her bedroom, she grabbed a towel from the bathroom. She lined the box with the towel and then gently removed the little kittens one by one from her jacket and placed them in the box.

Debra Sue thought, *They look so adorable and cute.* In reality, the kittens were not adorable and cute at all but were filthy and mangy looking. They were nothing but skin and bones.

Debra Sue knew the kittens were probably starving, so she went to the kitchen and poured some milk into a small saucer. She placed the saucer in the box and then dunked each kitten's face into the milk. The kittens started lapping up the milk.

After the kittens had lapped up all the milk, and their little tummies were all pooched out, Debra Sue shoved the box under her bed. Then she went to the bathroom and washed the cut on her leg and placed a Band-Aid over the cut. She was good as new and ran outside to play.

Later that day, Gwen came into the children's bedroom to clean it when she heard meowing coming from under Debra Sue's bed. She looked under the bed and pulled out the box of kittens.

Gwen smiled as she knew Debra Sue was at it again, always trying to save little animals. But she took one look at those mangy little kittens and knew she would have to take them to the pound.

Gwen hollered, "Debra Sue, get your butt in here right now!"

Debra Sue ran into the bedroom with a big grin on her face and said, "I saved the kittens. Can I keep them, Mommy?"

Gwen replied, "No. These kittens have the mange. You can get ringworm from handling these kittens. I'm going to take them to the pound where they can take care of them and give them to a good home. Where did you get these kittens from?"

Debra Sue replied, "I found them in the vacant house next door."

Gwen said, "You were a brave girl to go into a vacant home to save some animals. But don't ever go into vacant homes again. There could be snakes or spiders in them."

Debra Sue never thought about snakes or spiders being in the vacant home and said, "Yes, ma'am."

Sure enough, a couple days later, Gwen had to take Debra Sue to the doctor because she had ringworm. But that would not stop stubborn Debra Sue. Because of her big heart, she just could not help herself from trying to save all the stray animals or help any injured little animals that she came upon.

One warm and sunny day, Debra Sue and James were playing outside. They were both running around in the grass barefoot. At least Debra Sue's right foot was not wearing a shoe. She had to wear that ugly old shoe that was attached to her leg brace on her left foot. She loved the feeling of running around in the grass with her one bare foot.

Debra Sue decided they would kick a ball around and said, "James, go inside and get a ball from our room."

James said, "Okay," and walked inside to go get a ball.

While James went into the house, Debra Sue walked to the backyard fence where there was a vine growing. She was looking for some berries when she heard birds squawking. She looked to where the squawking was coming from and saw two baby birds lying helpless on the ground at the base of an oak tree.

The oak tree just happened to be in the backyard of the vacant home next door. Someone had burned some brush in that backyard earlier in the day, and there were several piles of hot embers scattered throughout the yard.

Now Debra Sue had been told not to go into the vacant house next door. But Debra Sue figured that it would be okay to walk into the backyard of the vacant house next door to save some little birdies.

So stubborn Debra Sue walked carefully over to the oak tree making sure she didn't step on the hot piles of embers. She bent down and picked up the two darling little birds. She carried them gently back to her bedroom and lay them on her bed.

Debra Sue found a shoebox in her mother's closet and then went outside and pulled out several handfuls of grass. She placed the grass inside the shoebox and then made a little dent in the grass with her fist. She admired her homemade bird's nest and thought, *This nest will make a fine home for my little birdies.*

Debra Sue carried the shoebox with the grass nest into her bedroom. The little birds were squawking for their mother to come feed them. Debra Sue picked them both up and placed them into their new nest and asked the birdies, "How do you like your new home?"

The little birds just kept squawking for their mother to come and feed them. Debra Sue took their squawking as a sign of their approval on their new home and said, "I thought you would like it. Now I'm going to find you some food."

Debra Sue went outside and started looking around for some caterpillars and ladybugs so she could feed them to her little birdies. Gwen looked out the window and saw Debra Sue crawling around on the ground looking for something.

Gwen opened the back door and asked, "What are you looking for, sweetie?"

Debra Sue replied, "I'm looking for food for my little birdies."

Gwen raised an eyebrow and asked, "What little birdies?"

Debra Sue grinned and replied, "My little birdies in my bedroom."

Gwen grimaced as she knew her daughter was at it again and was trying to save all the little animals in the world and said, "You can't keep baby birds away from their mother. They will die. You have to take the baby birds back to where you found them so they will live. Now go get the baby birds and take them back right now."

Debra Sue stood up and pooched out her bottom lip pouting as she walked behind her mother into her bedroom. Gwen picked up the shoebox with the two baby birds and handed them to Debra Sue.

Gwen sternly said, "Take them back to where you found them right now! The baby birds' mother is probably looking for them!"

Debra Sue argued, "The mother abandoned her baby birds. They will die without me taking care of them."

Gwen yelled, "Go! Right now!"

Debra Sue reluctantly walked outside carrying the shoebox of baby birds. As she was walking toward the oak tree, a blue jay suddenly swooped down at Debra Sue shrieking at her. Debra Sue screamed out in fear as she ducked. The blue jay flew up and looped back around and swooped back down again attacking Debra Sue for a second time.

Debra Sue shrieked out and dropped the shoebox carrying the baby birds on the ground. She had had enough of this attacking blue jay and ran toward her house.

As she was running toward her house, she didn't notice the pile of hot embers in front of her. Her right barefoot stepped right in the center of those hot embers severely burning the bottom of her right foot.

Debra Sue was crying as she entered the back door of her home.

Gwen asked, "What's wrong, sweetie?"

Debra Sue sobbed, "A bird attacked me when I took back the little birdies, and I burned my foot."

Gwen looked at the bottom of Debra Sue's foot and gasped. "That's a nasty burn."

Gwen picked up Debra Sue and carried her to the bathroom. She filled up the bathtub with water and gently washed the bottom of her foot. She then sprayed the bottom of Debra Sue's foot with antiseptic and then carried her to bed.

Gwen said, "You will have to stay off of your feet for a few days so your foot will not get infected."

Debra Sue said, "Okay, Mommy."

Gwen said, "From now on, I want you to wear shoes when you go outside. And I want you to stop bringing home all these stray animals you find. Okay, honey?"

Debra Sue replied, "Yes, ma'am."

But stubborn Debra Sue would continue to take home stray animals, clean them, feed them, and hide them under her bed to keep them safe. Once, Debra Sue even took home an animal that wasn't a stray.

The neighbor's dog had a litter of six puppies. When the litter of pups were six weeks old, the neighbor had let Debra Sue pet the puppies that were kept in the garage. Debra Sue thought the puppies were so cute. She thought they were so cute that she just had to have one. Debra Sue had seen the puppies' mother go in and out of the doggy door located on the bottom of the rear garage door.

So when the neighbor drove away from their home, Debra Sue walked over to the doggy door and crouched down on her hands and knees. She thought, *I think I can squeeze through the doggy door.* Debra Sue pushed on the doggy door, and it swung inward.

*Good. It's not locked,* Debra Sue thought, as she poked her head inside the doggie door. Then she squeezed her shoulders through the opening and then crawled the rest of the way into the garage. She picked up the cutest puppy she could find and carried it to the doggy door.

Debra crawling in a doggy door, illustrated by Chase & Kayla Tracey

She shoved the puppy out of the doggy door and said, "You stay right by the door, puppy."

Debra Sue squeezed out of the doggy door and picked up her cute little puppy and headed home. She walked into the kitchen and retrieved a bowl from the cupboard. She filled the bowl with milk and then carried the bowl of milk in one hand and puppy in the other into her bedroom.

Debra Sue set the bowl down at the foot of her bed and then dunked the puppy's face into the milk. While the puppy was lapping up the milk, she got a shoebox and lined it with a hand towel.

When the puppy finished lapping up all the milk, Debra Sue placed the puppy into the box and gently rubbed the puppy's back until it fell asleep. Then she hid the puppy in her closet and went outside to play. Gwen was fixing supper when the puppy awakened and started yipping loudly. Gwen marched into Debra Sue's bedroom thinking, *She's up to her old ways again.*

Gwen opened the bedroom door and heard the whining coming from the closet. She opened the closet door and saw the little puppy whining in the shoebox. Gwen hollered, "Debra Sue, get your butt in here right now!"

Debra Sue came running into the bedroom with a sheepish grin on her face and asked, "Can I keep my puppy, Mommy?"

Gwen sharply said, "No! Is this the neighbor's puppy?"

Debra Sue replied, "Yes, ma'am."

Gwen asked, "How did you get the puppy?"

Debra Sue lied and said, "The puppy must have crawled out of the doggy door."

Gwen said sharply, "You march yourself right over to the neighbor and give them their puppy back right now, young lady!"

Debra Sue said, "Yes, ma'am."

Debra Sue picked up her little puppy, pooched out her bottom lip, and pouted as she returned her puppy back to the neighbor. She thought, *They don't need all those puppies.*

The neighbor thanked Debra Sue and told her they were looking all over for their puppy.

Stubborn Debra Sue would continue to bring home stray animals, clean them, feed them, and hide them under her bed, in her closet, or in the garage. That would be until Gwen would find the strays, and out they would go.

## THE BICYCLE

WHEN SULLY WENT ON strike against the petroleum company, they were forced to sell their first house and move into a rental home. Gwen went to work as a waitress to help with the finances.

The strike finally ended, and Sully went back to work. Gwen decided to continue working as a waitress. However, the financial problems continued, and Sully fell behind on the rent and started to look for another rental home.

One evening at the dinner table, Sully said, "I'm looking for another place to live. We will be moving in a month or two."

After dinner, Debra Sue was helping Mom with the dishes. As she was drying a plate, Debra Sue asked, "Mom, why are we moving again?"

Gwen replied, "Money is tight right now. But don't worry. We'll be okay."

Since Sully was back at work and Gwen was working as a waitress, Debra Sue thought, *I must be the reason why Mom and Dad are poor. Mom is constantly running all over the place for me. She has to go to the brace maker to fix the straps. She has to go to the shoemaker to attach the shoe to the brace. She has to go back to the brace maker when I outgrow the braces. Then she has to go back to the shoemaker so he can attach a new shoe to the brace. I'm a burden on Mom and Dad. I wish I didn't need this leg brace. I'm the reason we are poor.*

It was September 1 when the family moved once again. Debra Sue would be going to another school and would have to make new friends. As Sully parked the car in the driveway, he said, "This is our new home, kids. Start unpacking."

Gwen was first out of the car and led the way toward the house. Debra Sue scrambled out of the car and followed close behind her mother. James, Terry, and Debra's other two sisters followed. Gwen unlocked the door and walked in.

Debra Sue walked into the house and started to check it out. This rental home had a large kitchen, large living room, den, three bedrooms, and two baths. When Debra Sue opened the back door, she saw a large backyard. She thought, *This is a much larger home than that two-bedroom home we had before. Maybe I can have a dog with this big backyard. I won't have to share a bedroom with my brother and all my sisters.* Debra Sue was getting older now, and she wanted a little privacy.

Sully started carrying all the boxes into the house.

Gwen gathered her children around her and said, "I'm going to show you your bedrooms."

Gwen led her children down the hallway. Gwen stopped by the first bedroom on the right and said, "This will be Debra Sue's and Terry's bedroom."

Stubborn Debra Sue pooched out her bottom lip pouting and said, "I don't get my own bedroom?"

Gwen irritated, sharply said, "No! You don't get your own bedroom! You're already getting the larger of the two bedrooms."

Stubborn Debra Sue stormed out and stomped into the living room. She could care less what her brother and other sisters room looked like. Gwen led the other children past the bathroom and showed them their bedroom on the right at the end of the hallway.

Gwen led the children back into the living room and said, "The master bedroom is your dad's and my bedroom. You kids stay out of our bedroom. Now let's go get the furniture and boxes into the house."

After all the furniture and boxes were brought inside and placed in the proper rooms, Debra Sue went outside to rest. She sat down on the grass and leaned against the tree in her front yard.

Debra Sue was watching a boy about her age riding his bike up and down the street. He looked over at Debra Sue and smiled and then waved hi. Debra Sue waved back at him.

The boy rode his bike up to the curb in front of Debra Sue. He got off his bike and laid it down in the yard, and he walked up to Debra Sue and asked, "What's your name?"

Debra Sue replied, "Debra. What's your name?"

The boy smiled and said, "My name is David. You sure are pretty."

Debra Sue felt her face blush as she said, "Thank you. I have to go unpack now," and started to stand up.

David said, "Let me help you," and offered his hand to help pull Debra Sue up.

Debra Sue took his hand and let him help her up and said, "Thank you."

David smiled that she was pleased and said, "No problem. See you later," and walked to his bike, picked it up, and rode down the street grinning from ear to ear.

As Debra Sue walked to the house she thought, *He sure embarrassed me when he called me pretty right to my face. That was nice of him to offer to help me up. He never stared at my leg brace or asked what was wrong with my leg. What was his name? David, I think.* When Debra Sue walked into the house, she hollered, "Mom! Will you buy me a bike?"

Gwen replied, "You don't know how to ride a bike."

Debra Sue asked, "If I learn how to ride a bike, will you buy me one?"

Gwen replied, "If you show me you can ride a bicycle, then yes, I will buy you a bike. Now go unpack your clothes in your bedroom."

Debra Sue screamed with delight, "All right! Thanks, Mom!" She ran to her bedroom with a big grin on her face and started unpacking her clothes. Debra Sue loved her new home.

The next Monday, after the family had moved into their rental home, it was time for Debra Sue to start school. Gwen kept up her tradition of taking Debra Sue to school on the very first day. Then Gwen would walk with Debra Sue into her classroom and then say her goodbye.

On the second day of school, while eating breakfast, Gwen dropped a bombshell and said, "Debra Sue, you live too far away from your school to walk, and I have to go to work early in the morning. So you will have to ride the school bus to school and back home when school lets out."

Now Debra Sue had never ridden a school bus before, and she panicked and started to cry. She stammered, "I...I...I've never ridden a school bus before. I'm too scared, Mom. Please take me to school."

Gwen reassuringly said, "I've talked to the school officials and the school bus supervisor. They will make sure you get on the right bus, and they will help you get on and off the bus. They will drop you off as close to our house as possible. You will be okay, sweetie."

Stubborn Debra Sue cried, "I'm sick. I don't want to go to school."

Gwen said, "You're just scared because this is the first time for riding a school bus. Kids your age ride the school bus all the time. You will be just fine. I'll help you get on the bus today."

When it was time for the school bus to arrive, Gwen took Debra Sue by the hand and walked her to the end of the block where the bus would stop. The school bus arrived five minutes later.

The bus driver was a nice lady and helped Debra Sue onto the bus and smiling said, "We left the front seat vacant just for you Debra Sue."

Debra Sue sat down on the front seat and hung her head down, trying to fight back her tears. Just then, the boy that lived across the street from her climbed onto the bus and said, "Can I sit next to you, Debra?"

Debra Sue looked up and was relieved to see a familiar face and thought, *What was his name? David, I think,* and said, "Okay."

David chattered the entire time, and before Debra Sue knew it, they were arriving at the school. The school bus parked and opened the door for the kids to exit. David stood up and said, "I'll help you off the bus."

Debra Sue said, "That's okay. I'm going to wait until everyone is off the bus before I get off. I'm too slow."

David said, "Okay. I'll wait with you," and he sat back down.

Debra Sue felt bad that David would have to wait to get off the bus because of her and said, "That's okay. You don't have to wait for me."

David said, "I want to wait for you."

After the last kid exited the bus, David stood up and said, "Now, it's our turn."

The bus driver stood up and smiled at David and said, "That was nice of you to wait for Debra Sue. You get off the bus, and I will help Debra Sue get off the bus."

When Debra Sue was off the school bus, David walked side by side with her into the school building. At the end of the school day, David waited at the school bus loading zone for Debra Sue.

When Debra Sue walked to the bus loading zone, David smiled and waved at her. The bus driver helped Debra Sue onto the bus, and David sat next to her on the first seat behind the bus driver. That was when Debra Sue became friends with him. David would be Debra Sue's first boyfriend.

On Saturday, Debra Sue went outside and saw David riding his bike up and down the street. As soon as David saw Debra Sue, he waved and rode over next to her.

Debra Sue asked, "Will you help me ride a bike?"

David was pleased that Debra Sue asked for his help and replied, "Sure."

He got off his bicycle and held it steady for Debra Sue. She grabbed the handlebars and then stood there a minute trying to figure out the best way to climb on the bicycle, with her awkward leg brace. She firmly planted her left leg with the brace and then swung her right leg over the bicycle.

She swung her leg over the bike too hard and her weight carried her too far over the bike and both her and the bicycle fell sideways. David was caught off guard and lost his grip as Debra Sue fell to the ground.

Debra Sue said, "I'm sorry."

Debra Sue's leg brace made it difficult for her to shove the bicycle off her. David bent over and lifted her leg brace off the bicycle, and then Debra Sue pushed the bike off her.

David asked, "Are you okay?"

Red faced with embarrassment but still determined, stubborn Debra Sue said, "I'm fine. Will you hold the bike again for me?"

David was pleased that a girl would still be asking for his help, even after he let her fall down and said, "Sure. No problem."

David held the bike steady. This time he was going to hold it with all his might. Debra Sue knew what she did wrong, and this time she held the handlebars and slowly lifted her right leg over the bike and pulled herself up onto the seat.

Debra Sue put her right foot on the pedal which was on the downside of the bike. Her left leg was straight because of the brace. Debra Sue said, "Push me to get me going."

David said, "Okay. Here we go," and started pushing her while holding onto the side of the bike. Debra Sue had to wait until the pedal rotated around until it was in the up position. Then she took her right foot and pushed the pedal down hard, and away she went. David let go of the bike as she took off.

There was no way her left leg could bend with the brace on, so Debra Sue kept her left leg out away from the pedal. The motion of the bicycle propelled the right pedal back to the up position, and Debra Sue pushed the pedal down hard again. She repeated the process and rode down the street. Every once in a while, her leg brace would hit the left pedal.

When Debra Sue rode to the end of the street, she realized she didn't know how to stop the bicycle. She stopped pedaling, and the bike slowed down. She saw a car parked on the side of the street, and Debra Sue decided to use the car to stop herself.

She grabbed the mirror on the side of the car door and leaned the bike against the car to stop. Debra Sue thought, *I sure hope the owner doesn't notice the little dent and scratch the bike made on the door.*

Debra Sue leaned the bike over so her brace leg could touch the ground. She swung her right leg off the bicycle and lost her balance. She fell to the pavement skinning her right knee and elbow. Stubborn Debra Sue didn't give up and picked herself up and then the bike. David ran up to her and asked, "Are you okay, Debra?"

Debra Sue replied, "I'm fine. How do you stop the bicycle?" David wanted to kick himself for not being a better teacher and explained, "You just push the pedal backward, and it will stop the bike."

Debra Sue said, "Oh, okay. Can I keep on riding to get better?" David said, "You sure can."

Debra Sue leaned the bicycle on a different car. She made sure the right pedal was in the up position as she climbed on the bike. She pushed down hard on the pedal, and off she went. As the pedal rotated back up, Debra Sue thought, *If that pedal doesn't come back up to the top, I'm going to be in a world of hurt.*

Debra Sue made sure she pushed down hard each time so the bicycle would move fast enough so the pedal would keep rotating back up to the top. One time, her foot slipped off the pedal, and she fell onto the bar at the top of the bicycle. She screamed out in pain, but stubborn Debra Sue didn't let that stop her from continuing to ride.

When Debra Sue was ready to stop the bike, she would look for something to grab onto when she slowed the bike down. She would grab on a car's side mirror, a light pole, or a stop sign. It was no wonder the owners of the cars would one day complain to Debra Sue's parents about all the dents and scratches on their cars.

Finally, David said, "It's my turn to ride my bicycle!"

Debra Sue said, "Okay," and rode up to a car parked by the curb, grabbed the mirror, and came to a halting stop. Debra Sue climbed off the bike and held it for David and said, "Thanks for teaching me how to ride a bicycle."

David smiled and said, "No problem," climbed on his bicycle, and rode down the street grinning from ear to ear.

A few weeks later, Terry was celebrating her sixth birthday. Her birthday was almost two weeks earlier than Debra Sue's birthday. Terry jumped up and down when she received a bicycle on her birthday.

Debra Sue pooched out her bottom lip with jealousy. Stubborn Debra Sue made an ugly remark to Terry, "You have a baby bicycle. It has to have training wheels."

Terry replied, "You're just jealous because you don't have a bicycle."

Terry climbed onto her bicycle with training wheels and rode up and down the street, laughing the entire time.

David came outside and started riding his bicycle up and down the street with Terry. Stubborn Debra Sue became angry that David was riding his bicycle with Terry and hollered, "Hi, David. What are you doing?"

David hollered back, "Hi, Debra," and rode his bicycle away from Terry and rode up to Debra Sue and stopped.

Debra Sue smiled slyly and asked, "Can I show my mom that I know how to ride a bicycle?"

David replied, "Okay."

Debra Sue said, "Thank you." She ran into the house and hollered, "Mom, come watch me ride a bicycle."

Gwen nearly dropped the dishes she was carrying into the kitchen in disbelief and said, "Okay, honey."

Debra Sue ran outside and leaned the bicycle against the car making sure the right pedal was in the up position. She climbed on the bike and pushed the pedal down hard with the right leg and kept the left leg with the brace stuck out to the side, making sure it wouldn't hit the left pedal.

Debra Sue was off and riding the bicycle. She had managed the art of turning the bike around at the end of the street without stopping. She pedaled the bicycle with her good leg only and headed back toward her mother.

Gwen gasped with excitement as she saw her little girl riding a bicycle. She clapped, whooped, and hollered as Debra Sue rode toward her. Debra Sue slowed the bike down and grabbed the mirror on the car door in the driveway and came to a halting stop.

Gwen said, "Stay right there. I'm going to go get the camera and take a picture of you riding the bike."

David ran over to Debra Sue and said, "Okay. It's my turn to ride."

Debra Sue said, "My mom went to get a camera. Can I ride it so she can take a picture of me riding a bicycle?"

David said, "Okay."

Debra Sue said, "Will you help me turn the bike around?"

David replied, "Okay," and helped Debra Sue get off the bike and turned it around to face the street. Debra Sue made sure the right pedal was in the up position and then leaned the bike against the car and climbed onto it. She was ready to head down the driveway and onto the street.

Gwen ran out of the house out of breath and said, "Okay, sweetie. Start riding the bike and I will take some pictures."

Debra Sue said, "Mom, just take pictures on my right side when I ride the bicycle. I don't want anyone to see my leg brace."

Gwen said, "Don't be silly, Debra Sue."

Stubborn Debra Sue hollered, "I mean it, Mom! Or I won't ride the bicycle so you can take pictures!"

Gwen said, "Okay. Okay. Now start riding your bicycle, sweetie."

Debra Sue pushed down hard on the right pedal, and off she went down the driveway and onto the street. Gwen took several pictures to show proof that her little girl could ride a bicycle in spite of having to wear a full leg brace.

Debra Sue rode down the street and then back up the street and into her driveway. She grabbed a hold of the mirror on the side of the car and came to a quick halt. She climbed off the bike with a big grin on her face and said, "I learned how to ride a bike. Will you buy me a bike now?"

Gwen said, "Right now, money is tight. But we'll try to get you one."

Debra Sue ran over to David, patted him on the back, and said, "Thank you for teaching me how to ride a bike."

David smiled and said, "You're welcome."

David climbed on his bike and rode down the driveway and onto the street grinning from ear to ear. He was pleased that his girlfriend gave him a pat on the back. He was looking forward to getting his first kiss from Debra Sue.

At supper, Gwen informed Sully of Debra Sue's feat of riding a bike. Sully said, "That's my tough soldier girl. When she sets her mind to doing something, she will figure out a way to do it."

Even though money was tight, Gwen kept her promise. She purchased a used girl's bicycle from a secondhand store. When Debra Sue celebrated her ninth birthday, Gwen rolled the bicycle from the garage and said, "Happy birthday, Debra Sue."

Stubborn Debra Sue looked at her bicycle in disbelief. Her bicycle was a used, old looking, ugly gray girl's bicycle. She tried her hardest to give a weak smile and said, "Thank you, Mom."

Gwen said, "I love you, sweetie. Happy birthday."

Debra Sue said, "This bicycle doesn't have a bar at the top like the one I rode yesterday."

Gwen said, "No, honey. That was a boy's bike. This is a girl's bicycle."

Debra Sue said, "This will be a lot easier to ride, and I won't hurt myself if my foot slips off the pedal. Thanks, Mom"

Gwen raised an eyebrow not knowing quite what to think about her comment. But before she could say anything, Debra Sue leaned the bicycle against the car with the right pedal in the up position, climbed on the bike, and off she went riding down the street.

Gwen yelled, "Debra Sue, come back here! I want to take some pictures of you riding your bike."

Debra Sue grumbled and turned her bicycle around and rode back to the house. Debra Sue yelled, "Don't take pictures of my leg brace, Mom!"

Gwen said, "Don't be silly."

Stubborn Debra Sue yelled, "I mean it, Mom!"

Gwen said, "Okay. I won't take any pictures of your leg brace."

Now when it came to taking pictures, Debra Sue's sister Terry loved being in the spotlight. She started jumping up and down and yelling, "Take a picture with me riding with Debra Sue, Mom!"

Gwen said, "That's a great idea. Come over here, Debra, and let your sister ride with you on your new bicycle."

Debra Sue pooched out her bottom lip pouting and said, "No. Terry can ride her own bicycle. She doesn't have to butt in on my bicycle."

Gwen said, "Just this one time for a picture. Get over here right now!"

Debra Sue pulled up in the driveway and turned the bicycle around so it was heading out to the street. Debra Sue gave a mean look at Terry and said, "Get on behind me. You always have to be the center of attention. Don't you, Terry?"

Terry was grinning from ear to ear as she climbed on the back of the bicycle and held on tight to Debra Sue.

Debra Sue gave a sly smirk and lied, "I can't get the bicycle going with Terry sitting on the back."

Gwen said, "Don't worry," and hollered, "James, come over here and help your sisters out and give them a push on the bicycle! That way I can get a picture of all three of you with the new bicycle."

James was always willing to help his mother and sisters out and politely said, "Yes, ma'am." James came running over and started pushing his sisters on the bicycle, while Gwen clicked away on the camera. Away Debra Sue and Terry went down the yard and into the street, riding her new used bicycle.

Debra, Terry, and James on a bike

Stubborn Debra Sue had learned how to ride a bicycle in spite of having a full leg brace that kept her from bending her left leg. Debra Sue proved that where there is a will, there is a way.

A month later, Debra Sue was invited to David's birthday party at the skating rink. When Debra Sue saw everyone skating, she asked her mom, "Can I go roller-skating?"

Gwen replied, "You don't know how to skate. You'll fall down and hurt yourself, and you might break your brace."

Stubborn Debra Sue said, "I learned how to ride a bike. I can learn how to roller skate. Please let me roller skate, Mom."

Gwen said, "Sweetie, your shoe is attached to your brace. You have to wear a roller skate. I don't think a roller skate can fit over your shoe that's attached to your brace."

Gwen looked at Debra Sue's pitiful begging eyes, and then she gave in and said, "Let's see if we can find some roller skates that can fit over your shoe on your brace."

Gwen asked the manager if they could rent two pair of roller skates. One for her right foot and a much larger one to fit over her brace. The manager was very kind and found a huge roller skate that barely fit over Debra Sue's leg brace. He only charged them for one pair of roller skates.

Debra Sue was grinning from ear to ear as she shuffled to the skating floor holding onto the wall. She stepped on the floor, and two steps later, Debra Sue's butt was on the floor. Gwen picked her up off the floor and held her hand as she kept her feet about a foot apart. Debra Sue let her mom pull her on her skates.

Debra Sue watched how the other kids moved their feet back and forth to skate across the floor. As Gwen held her hand, Debra Sue started moving her legs back and forth, and she started slowly skating. Although it was difficult for Debra Sue to skate with her leg brace, she said, "Let go of my hand, Mom."

Gwen said, "Okay, sweetie. I'll be right by your side." Gwen let go of Debra Sue's hand, and she skated two feet and fell down.

David saw Debra Sue fall down, and he immediately came skating over to her rescue. David asked, "Are you okay, Debra?"

Debra Sue replied, "I'm okay."

Gwen started to pick her up when stubborn Debra Sue said, "I can get up on my own, Mom."

Gwen let her struggle on own as she stood up leaning wobbly against the wall. Debra Sue steadied herself and then held one hand on the wall and pushed herself forward.

Debra Sue was skating on her own. Eventually, Debra Sue let go of the wall and was skating by herself. David would come over and hold her hand while they would skate around the rink. Debra Sue had the time of her life. Gwen sat a table and couldn't believe her little girl was roller-skating.

Ever since Debra Sue was an infant, she would figure out a way to accomplish her goal. Stubborn Debra Sue never quit, and she never gave up, proving that where there is a will, there is a way.

## FRIENDSHIPS

DEBRA SUE LIVED ON a street that looked like a horseshoe and ran by the park behind her house. Debra Sue was getting to be an old pro at riding her bicycle. She started to ride her bike farther and farther.

One day, Debra Sue was feeling brave as she rode her bicycle down to the intersection. Instead of turning around at the intersection, she turned right on the next street.

Debra Sue continued past the park and pedaled through the curve onto the next street. Debra Sue pedaled on and then made another right turn back onto the street where she lived. Debra Sue thought, *Now that was a blast,* and decided to do it again.

Debra Sue pedaled faster and flew past her house. She pedaled toward the intersection and made the right turn. She was going a little too fast and ended up on the wrong side of the street.

Thank goodness, no cars were coming, or it could have been disastrous. Debra Sue thought, *I'll have to slow down when I turn at the intersections from now on.*

From that day on, Debra Sue would constantly ride her bicycle around the horseshoe-shaped street that ran past the park. Some days, she would ride her bicycle alongside David. Some days, she would ride her bicycle with her sister, Terry. But Terry wasn't allowed to ride her bicycle on the street. Terry always had to ride her bicycle on the sidewalk.

One day, a girl was standing in the front yard on the next street and waved hi as Debra Sue rode past her. Debra Sue waved back and kept on riding.

As Debra Sue was making her second trip around the horse-shoe-shaped street, the girl was standing at the curb and hollered, "What's your name?"

Debra Sue stopped her bicycle in front of her and said, "Debra. What's your name?"

The girl replied, "Nancy. I've been seeing you ride your bicycle all the time. I wanted to meet you. Would you like to come to my house and play with my dolls sometime?"

Nancy didn't stare at Debra Sue's leg brace, and she never asked what was wrong with her leg. Debra Sue thought, *Nancy sees me as a normal person and not as a handicapped person.* Debra Sue said, "I'll ask my mom. Maybe you can come to my house and play with my dolls too."

That would be the start a long friendship. In fact, Nancy would be Debra Sue's best girlfriend. Debra Sue and Nancy would go over to each other homes and play with their dolls for hours and hours. Even their mothers got to know each other and often had morning coffee together.

It was Nancy's birthday, and she wanted a slumber party. Nancy and her mom came over to Debra Sue's house and asked Gwen, "We would like to invite Debra Sue over for a slumber party tonight for Nancy's birthday. There's going to be about ten girls there."

Gwen said, "That sounds like a lot of fun. Of course, she can go."

Debra Sue and Nancy screamed with delight, jumping up and down. Debra Sue said, "I'll pack my pajamas."

Debra Sue's sister, Terry was always trying to tag along with her big sister and Terry hollered, "I want to go too!"

Debra Sue yelled, "No! Nancy is my friend, and you are not tagging along!"

Nancy's Mom said, "Well, of course, Terry can come along. The more, the merrier in a slumber party. It'll be a blast."

Debra Sue argued, "Mom! Tell Terry she can't go with me! It's my slumber party, not Terry's!"

Gwen said, "Sure, Terry can go," and thought, *Now I can have some peace and quiet.*

Terry jumped up and down with joy. Stubborn Debra Sue pooched out her bottom lip and pouted. As Debra Sue and Terry were packing their pajamas, Debra Sue shoved Terry away from her and said, "You always have to butt in."

Terry stuck out her tongue at Debra Sue and said, "I want to have fun too."

Debra Sue, Nancy, and Nancy's mom headed toward the car with Terry tagging along behind them. Now Nancy's mother was something else. Maybe even a little on the wild side.

When all the girls arrived at the house for the slumber party, Nancy said, "Okay, kids. We're going to have a scavenger hunt. There will be three girls in each group. Each group has to go get the items on your list. You can go to the houses up and down on this street only. We'll meet back at the house in thirty minutes."

Nancy's mom assigned Debra Sue, Nancy, and Terry into one group. Then she assigned the other girls into their groups. Nancy's mom gave each group their list. The list contained items like gum, apple, cookies, popcorn, jar of pickles, and toilet paper. Then she said, "Okay, let's go get the items on the list."

As Debra Sue, Nancy, and Terry walked toward the first house, Debra Sue said, "Your mom sure is cool and fun." Debra Sue had a blast going house to house asking for the items on the list. When all the groups arrived back at the house with the items on their scavenger list, everyone placed their items on the living room floor. Debra Sue noticed that everyone had toilet paper on their list. There were ten rolls of toilet paper on the living room floor.

Nancy's mom said, "Oh, my goodness! Look at all this toilet paper. We need to get rid of it. Is anyone up to wrapping a house with toilet paper?"

Nancy laughed and screamed, "I am!"

Debra Sue giggled and sheepishly said, "Okay," and again thought, *Nancy's mom sure is cool. She is a lot of fun. I wish my mom was that cool.*

Nancy's mom said, "Okay. Everyone in the car. I know a house we can wrap."

Everyone ran and climbed into the car. Several of the girls sat on each other's laps. Debra Sue was getting a little nervous now. She didn't really think Nancy's mom would go and wrap a house. But before she knew it, they were on their way to wrap a house.

Nancy's mom drove around for a bit and finally pointed to a house and said, "There. That looks like a good house to wrap."

She parked the car by the curb one house down from the one she pointed at. She asked all the girls, "Do you all have your toilet paper?"

Everyone laughed and said, "Yes."

Nancy's mom said, "Okay. Go over to the tree in the front yard and throw your roll of toilet paper as high as you can into the tree."

All the girls climbed out of the car and walked quietly to the tree. Debra Sue's heart was pounding as she was about to commit her first crime.

All the other girls started throwing their roll of toilet paper as high as they could into the tree and started laughing. Just as Debra Sue was throwing her roll of toilet paper into the tree, the front door opened and a woman hollered, "Hey! What are you doing!"

All of a sudden, several big girls came running out of the door, down the porch, and toward the girls. All the other girls screamed and started running back toward the car.

Debra Sue screamed in terror as she turned around and ran. Her heart felt like it was beating out of her chest as all the other girls were passing her by. Debra Sue's leg brace would only allow her to run so fast. She just knew she was going to get caught and go to prison.

Debra Sue looked toward the car, hoping that Nancy's mom would come and rescue her. But all she saw was Nancy's mom doubled over with laughter. Then Debra Sue realized the big girls chasing them were laughing also.

Nancy's mom had pulled a big prank on all the slumber party girls. Nancy's oldest sister was having a party at the house they were wrapping. Nancy's mom had told her oldest daughter to run out of the house with her friends and scare the girls when they start throwing the toilet paper up into the tree.

Nancy's mom's prank worked. It scared the dickens out of Debra Sue. But Debra Sue still thought Nancy's mom was really cool and fun.

Debra Sue, Nancy, and David started hanging out together. They would ride their bicycles up and down the street together constantly. Debra Sue became very proficient at riding her bicycle. Whenever Debra Sue did not push the right pedal down hard enough for the right pedal to return back to the top, she would take her heel and pull the pedal back up. One day, David noticed Debra Sue taking her heel and pulling the pedal back up from time to time. David was amazed at how Debra Sue would figure things out and said, "Debra, you sure are smart. I'm going to marry you."

Debra Sue blushed and said, "Don't be silly."

A short time later, Debra Sue said, "I'm tired. I'm going inside now."

David said, "Okay. I am going to marry you."

David ran into his house and hollered, "Mom. I'm going to marry Debra."

David's mom said, "How are you going to afford to take care of Debra?"

David said, "What do you mean? How I am going to afford to take care of her?"

David's mom said, "It costs money to take care of a girl. You have to buy them new clothes and makeup and stuff like that. Maybe you better wait until you are a little older and you get yourself a job."

David said, "Okay. But I'm going to marry Debra."

David's mom said, "Okay."

The next day when David was riding with Debra Sue, he told Debra Sue what his mom had told him and said, "When I get older and get a job, I'm going to marry you."

Debra Sue said, "Okay, that makes sense," and thought, *Thank goodness his mom talked some sense into his head. I'm not about to marry him at my age, silly boy.*

Debra Sue had thought that David and she were just friends. But David wanted to be more than just friends. He was more serious and wanted to marry her. David did not see Debra Sue as a handicapped person. David was a true friend.

Now Nancy was Debra Sue's best friend, and they would be best friends for many years to come. Until the day would come when Nancy would severely hurt Debra Sue's feelings. On that day, there was a party at the Strawberry Park's swimming pool. Nancy saw a nice-looking boy and told Debra Sue, "I have a crush on him."

Debra Sue replied, "I don't blame you. He's cute," and thought, *She's following him around like a little puppy dog. It's obvious he's not interested in her.*

After the pool party, everyone loaded up into the station wagon and headed home. Nancy quickly climbed in behind her new boyfriend when he and two of his friends climbed into the very back of the station wagon. Debra Sue and four other kids crammed into the back seat of the station wagon, and three other kids sat in the front seat.

On the drive home, Debra Sue overheard Nancy's new boyfriend ask, "Who's that pretty girl you were with at the swimming pool?"

Nancy replied loud enough for Debra Sue to hear, "You don't want to meet her. She's crippled."

Debra Sue couldn't believe her best friend would say something so cruel, as she fought back tears. That would forever end her friendship with Nancy.

Debra Sue had thought that Nancy and she were best friends. Debra Sue never considered herself as being handicapped and couldn't believe her best friend would call her a cripple. Debra Sue couldn't understand why her best friend would make fun of her. Nancy saw her as a handicapped person and just used her. Nancy was not a true friend at all.

Debra Sue found out what true friendships are all about at a young age.

## PAPER DOLLS AND A PICKLE

EVERY FRIDAY, DEBRA SUE received fifty-cents allowance for doing her chores and keeping her room clean. Debra Sue made sure she always completed all her chores and kept her room spotless so that she would receive her fifty-cents allowance.

As soon as Debra Sue received her allowance, she would dash across the street to the corner store. She would go straight to the magazine rack and look for a magazine that contained cut-out paper dolls. The magazine also had fashionable paper outfits with little tabs that you had to cut out with a pair of scissors.

Once Debra Sue found the magazine she liked the best, she would take it to the store clerk and lay her fifty cents on the counter. The store clerk would give her a nickel back in change. There was a big jar of pickles that cost a nickel sitting on the counter by the cash register. Every once in a while, Debra Sue would pocket the nickel, but most of the time, she would buy a big crunchy pickle. Debra Sue loved pickles.

Then she would leave the corner store and wait for the traffic light to flash the walking sign. Once the walking sign started flashing, Debra Sue would cross the street carrying her precious magazine in one hand and a pickle in the other.

One Friday when Debra Sue was standing at the corner store's magazine rack, she came across a thick paper doll magazine. This issue had double the dolls and double the fashionable outfits. She quickly picked up the magazine before anyone else could grab this to-die-for magazine.

Debra Sue took the magazine to the store clerk and laid her fifty cents on the counter like usual. This time the store clerk took the fifty cents but did not give Debra Sue a nickel back.

Debra Sue asked, "I don't get a nickel back so I can buy a pickle?"

The store clerk replied, "No. This magazine cost more than the other ones. Do you still want it?"

Debra Sue replied, "Yes, sir. I don't need a pickle."

The magazine actually cost seventy cents, but since Debra Sue was such a loyal customer, the store clerk let her have it for fifty cents. Debra Sue gently picked up her magazine off the counter and walked out of the corner store.

While waiting for the traffic light to flash the walking sign, Debra Sue became so excited for getting not only one, but two cut-out paper dolls, that she couldn't wait any longer to see her little paper dolls. She opened up her magazine and her imagination took over, and she started talking to her little dolls.

Debra Sue looked at the paper doll on the left side of the page and said, "Your name is Susie," and then she looked at the paper doll on the right side of the page and said, "Your name is Ella Mae. Susie, you are going to wear a dress when we go shopping. Ella Mae you are going to wear a blouse and jeans. You are just too hard on your clothes. You don't take care of them like Susie does."

Then Debra Sue caught a glimpse of a woman standing behind her and looking over her shoulder listening to her conversation with her paper dolls. Debra Sue felt her face get beet red from embarrassment and quickly shut her magazine and started humming,

"Dee...dee...da...dee...dee...do. Dee...dee...do...da."

The walking sign started flashing, and Debra Sue started walking as quickly as her heavy leg brace would let her go. Debra Sue thought, *That was so embarrassing having that woman watch me talking to my paper dolls like they were my children. I am so humiliated.*

When Debra Sue got into the privacy of her bedroom, her conversation with her little dolls continued. She dressed up Susie in a fashionable dress and then dressed up Ella Mae in a fashionable blouse and pair of jeans. Debra Sue loved to dress up her paper dolls with all the latest fashions.

After a while, Debra Sue got the urge to eat some pickles. She loved munching on pickles when she played with her paper dolls. She loved the way the pickles would make her mouth pucker up. Debra Sue thought, *I wish I had a nickel left over when I bought this magazine so I could buy a pickle at the store.*

Debra Sue ran into the kitchen and opened the refrigerator door. To her dismay, there was no jar of pickles. She thought for a while, then went to her bedroom, got a pencil and sheet of paper, and sat down at her little table.

On top of the paper, she wrote in capital letters "SCAVENGER HUNT." Under the title, she wrote a list of items and then drew a line through all of the items except for one.

That way, it would look like she had collected everything on the scavenger list except for that one item not having a line drawn through it. The items on the list that had a line drawn through it were toilet paper, pencil, apple, and gum. The only item on the list without a line drawn through it was a jar of pickles.

Debra Sue went into her closet and pulled out an old Easter basket. She went to the bathroom and placed a roll of toilet paper into the basket.

Then Debra Sue ran outside and handed the basket with the toilet paper and the scavenger list to her sister Terry and said, "Go to the brown house two doors down and knock on the door. When someone comes to the door, tell them you are on a scavenger hunt, and you need the last item on your list. Then give them your list."

Terry said, "No. You go."

Debra Sue coaxed her sister and said, "You're cuter. They will give you the jar of pickles. You know how you love pickles," and then gave Terry a gentle nudge to get her on her way.

Terry reluctantly said, "Okay," and walked to the brown house two doors down the street carrying the basket with the toilet paper sticking out.

Debra Sue hid behind the house peeking around the corner as she watched Terry go to the house down the street and knock on the door. Debra Sue giggled when she saw a woman open the door and take the list from her sister's hand.

The woman left with the note in her hand, and a short time later, she returned. She handed back the note with a jar of pickles to Terry. Terry ran back home with a huge grin on her face.

Terry said, "The lady gave me a jar of pickles and said I could cross off the last item on the list."

Debra Sue opened the jar of pickles, and they started laughing and giggling as they munched on their pickles. Debra Sue's plan had worked as she contentedly returned to her bedroom and continued playing with her paper dolls. Debra Sue gave new meaning to the phrase "Where there is a will, there is a way."

*Chapter 13*

---

## CERTIFIED SWIMMER

---

GWEN HOLLERED, "ARE YOU all packed and ready to go?"

Debra Sue was grinning from ear to ear as she replied, "I sure am, Mom."

Debra Sue was going on her very first summer camp excursion. Gwen picked up Debra Sue's suitcase and carried it to the car, with Debra Sue following close behind. They were both very excited and chatted constantly on the long drive.

Debra Sue quickly made new friends at the camp. The girls had their own dormitory, and the boys had their own dormitory. Debra Sue was having a blast at summer camp. They were doing all kinds of events. They roasted marshmallows at the campfire just before retiring to bed at night. Debra Sue even made a pot holder for her mom.

On the third day of the camp, everyone went to the Olympic-size pool to go swimming. The team leader who was assigned to Debra Sue's group led the way. The swimming pool was roped off, dividing it into three sections. The pool was designated for advanced swimmers, regular swimmers, and beginner swimmers.

Debra Sue walked up to the team leader and said, "I don't know how to swim."

The team leader said, "Don't worry. I'll teach you how to swim. You will be in group A with me for all of the beginners. Grab my hand and I'll walk with you as we go into the water."

Debra Sue was excited that she was going to learn how to swim. The team leader held Debra Sue's hand as she stepped into the water until she was waist deep. The team leader showed Debra Sue how to dog-paddle. Debra Sue splashed about and then sank under the water, getting water up her nose. She jumped up coughing and snorting water out of her nose.

The team leader laughed and said, "You're doing great. Now cup your hands and act like a puppy dog moving your hands and feet forward and backward," and then he demonstrated how to dog-paddle. Debra Sue tried to follow his instructions and started splashing around moving her hands and feet.

Stubborn Debra Sue would not give up. Even though she went under the water several times and had to cough and snort the water from her nose, she kept splashing about. After about thirty minutes, Debra Sue had dog-paddled about five feet.

The team leader clapped his hands and whooped and hollered and yelled, "All right! You're dog-paddling, Debra Sue!"

The last two days at summer camp, Debra Sue practiced swimming in the pool. She became so good, that on the last day of summer camp, she swam in the section designated for regular swimmers.

When everyone finished swimming, the team leader presented Debra Sue with a plastic card that stated Certified Swimmer. Debra Sue was so proud of her Certified Swimmer's card, she stuck it in her front pocket. She was now an official swimmer.

When Gwen arrived to pick up Debra Sue from summer camp, she couldn't even get out of the car before Debra Sue shoved her Certified Swimmer's card in her face and excitedly said, "I'm a certified swimmer, Mom." She was so excited, she almost forgot to give her mother the pot holder she had made for her.

On the way home, Debra Sue was chatting about everything she did at camp. She kept bringing up the fact that she was a certified swimmer. Debra Sue said, "I can't wait to go to Strawberry Park's swimming pool."

Stubborn Debra Sue kept pestering her mother to take her to Strawberry Park so she could go swimming. Gwen finally said she would take Debra Sue to the park on Monday, just to shut her up. Finally, Monday came, and Gwen kept her word and took Debra Sue to Strawberry Park so she could go swimming.

There were some kids Debra Sue's age diving off the high diving board. Debra Sue looked at her mother and said, "Mom, I'm going to dive off the high diving board into the deep end."

Gwen sternly said, "No! That's too dangerous!"

Stubborn Debra Sue pulled out her plastic card that stated "Debra Sue is a Certified Swimmer" and shoved it in Gwen's face and said, "I'm a certified swimmer. I want to be like all the other kids my age and jump off the high diving board."

Gwen wanted her daughter to feel confident about herself and hesitantly said, "I have to show the lifeguard your Certified Swimmer card. If he okays you to swim in the deep end, then you can dive off the high diving board. But you be very careful and hold on to the rails at the top of the diving board."

Debra Sue screamed with delight and said, "Okay," and gave Gwen her Certified Swimmer card.

Debra Sue watched her mother take her card to the lifeguard. The lifeguard read the card that stated "Debra Sue is a Certified Swimmer." He told Gwen that Debra Sue could swim in the deep end of the pool. Gwen nodded okay and motioned for Debra Sue to go to the high diving board.

Debra Sue placed her left hand above her left knee and headed toward the high diving board. She walked right past the low diving board without giving it a second glance. Debra Sue was smiling as she started climbing up the high diving board.

Her smile disappeared as she reached the top step, and her fear of heights set in. She thought, *It didn't look this high from the ground.* Debra Sue grabbed the handrails tightly as she stepped slowly toward the end of the diving board. Finally, she ran out of the handrails to hold on to. She had about three feet to go before she reached the end of the diving board.

Now Debra Sue was getting really nervous. She didn't want to let go of the handrails. She stood motionless, waiting to get up the nerve to take the last three steps.

She placed her hand above her left knee to keep it from buckling and took a step. The diving board started to sway up and down just a little. Debra Sue froze with fear. It was a miracle her left leg didn't buckle and cause her to fall to the pavement.

Debra Sue looked down at her mother for some encouragement. What she saw was her mother and the lifeguard both staring up at her with their mouths wide open in disbelief and shock. Debra Sue didn't want to disappoint her mother, after she did all that bragging about being a certified swimmer and could swim in the deep end of the pool.

Debra Sue took a deep breath and said, "Ah, the heck with it," and put her hand over her knee and headed toward the end of the diving board. The diving board started to sway after her first step, and Debra Sue quickly took her final step and dove forward.

Debra Sue was thankful she landed in the water and almost ignored the chilly water as she dived toward the bottom of the pool. However, the chilly water took her breath away, and she gasped for air as she reached the surface.

Debra Sue quickly swam to the edge of the pool and climbed out. She wrapped her body with a towel and sat on the pool deck. Her body was shaking from fear and the chilly water. Debra Sue thought, *I'm never getting on a diving board again.*

Then next year, Debra Sue was just as excited to go summer camp as she was the first time. Again, they had arts and crafts days, roasted marshmallows by the campfire, and on the third day, went to the Olympic-size swimming pool.

Debra Sue went straight to the regular swimmer's section and started swimming with her friends. Two lifeguards came over to Debra Sue, and one of them said, "You need to go to the beginner's section."

Debra Sue stood up and said, "I have a Certified Swimmer card."

The other lifeguard asked, "Who gave you a Certified Swimmer card?"

Debra Sue looked around and pointed to her team leader and said, "He trained me how to swim last year when I was here."

The two lifeguards started laughing and said, "He's not a lifeguard. He's just a team leader. I can't believe he gave you a Certified

Swimmer card. Especially the way you're splashing and flopping around like a fish out of water. You have to go to the beginner section of the pool." Stubborn Debra Sue refused to go to the beginner section of the pool. The lifeguards kept laughing and making fun of Debra Sue as she swam to the edge of the pool.

She climbed out of the pool, acting like they didn't bother her. Outside, she was smiling, but inside, she was so humiliated by the lifeguards laughing at how she was swimming. She had to fight back the tears as she walked to her dormitory.

Once she was inside her dormitory, she sat down on her bed and started to cry. About ten minutes later, a team leader saw Debra Sue in the dormitory and said, "You have to get outside and go swimming."

Debra Sue knew that girls on their menstrual periods didn't have to go swimming. All they had to say was, "I'm having a female day." Therefore, Debra Sue said, "I'm having a female day."

The team leader raised an eyebrow and knew Debra Sue was lying and thought, *She is not old enough to be having periods.* The team leader only replied, "Okay. But you should still get outside and enjoy the warm day."

Debra Sue walked out to the pool side deck and took a lounge chair. She sunbathed the last two days of camp. Debra Sue couldn't wait to go home. When Gwen pulled up, Debra Sue put her suitcase in the back of the car and climbed into the front seat and said, "Let's go home, Mom."

On the drive home, Gwen could tell Debra Sue was upset and asked, "What's wrong, sweetie?"

Debra Sue started crying and said, "The lifeguards were laughing and making fun of the way I was swimming. They said I was like a fish flopping around out of water. They said I wasn't a certified swimmer, and I had to swim in the beginner section of the pool. I told them I was a certified swimmer, but they still said I had to swim in the beginner section. I hate them. I'm never going back to summer camp again."

Gwen was livid at the way the lifeguards treated her little girl. She tried to ease Debra Sue's hurt feelings and said, "Don't you listen to those stupid lifeguards! You do know how to swim! Remember when you dove off the high diving board at Strawberry Park? You dove into the deep end of the pool and then swam to the edge of the pool. You are a certified swimmer."

Debra Sue remembered diving off the high diving board into the deep end of the pool, and then she swam to the edge of pool. Debra Sue felt better and exclaimed, "Yeah, I am a certified swimmer!"

# The Ankle Surgery

When Debra Sue started junior high school, she had to deal with a new set of obstacles, like how to keep up with the other classmates when walking up and down the stairs. She had to figure out the most efficient way to walk up and down the stairs.

Whenever Debra Sue walked up or down a flight of stairs, she had a fear of falling. She had to make sure there was a handrail to hold on to. Even if it meant going on the wrong side of the stairs.

When Debra Sue was going up the stairs, she had to lift her right leg up to the next higher step first. Then with her left hip, she would lift her left leg with the heavy brace up onto the same step. Then repeat the process, walking up the stairs one step at a time.

When Debra Sue was going down the stairs, she would have to lower her left leg with the heavy brace down first and then step down with her right leg. She would repeat the process, walking down the stairs one step at a time. This was a slow and exhausting process for Debra Sue and made it very difficult to keep up with her classmates.

The students knew Debra Sue would be slow in going up and down the stairs, so they would walk faster and sometimes even trot to get past her before she reached the stairs.

Sometimes the students would be so determined to pass Debra Sue they would inadvertently bump into her and cause her to fall down. Debra Sue would become red-faced with embarrassment and get up as quickly as she could and act as if nothing ever happened. She hated her leg brace for slowing her down.

Debra Sue's science class was upstairs, and the teacher was always taking the class outside in the spring. He would lead the students down the stairs and then outside. To avoid getting stuck behind Debra Sue, her classmates would quickly pass by Debra Sue before she reached the stairs. The stairs had ten steps, then there was a large landing, and then the stairs continued on down for another ten steps to the main floor. Debra Sue started walking down the stairs one step at a time. As the students were leaving her behind, she decided to skip the last step and jumped to the landing. She landed hard, and the brace bruised her pelvis. Debra Sue ignored the pain and continued down the remaining steps.

The students had left her behind. The teacher was either ignorant or uncaring about leaving a handicapped student behind. This time, stubborn Debra Sue decided to skip the last two steps on the stairs and jumped to the main floor. Again, she landed hard, and this time the strap on her leg brace broke. Debra Sue fell hard to the floor.

The other students had already exited the school and didn't even notice she had fallen. Debra Sue's embarrassment for falling was more concerning to her than her bruised knee, and she quickly pulled herself up.

Since her knee strap was broken, Debra Sue had to place her left hand on her knee to keep it from buckling when walking. She walked as fast as she could to the exit. She finally caught up with the rest of her classmates who were gathered around a large oak tree.

Stubborn Debra Sue would continue to try to keep up with her classmates. She was always skipping the last two steps on the stairs when she jumped to the floor. And she was always breaking the straps on her brace.

Today was no different. Only today, Debra Sue fell so far behind her classmates that stubborn Debra Sue decided to skip the last three steps and jumped to the floor. She landed so hard, that she broke the metal strip that connected to the knee part of the brace. Debra Sue was unable to get up.

A teacher saw Debra Sue lying on the floor and ran over to help her. He carried her to the nurse's office. The nurse called Gwen at her work to come pick Debra Sue up. Twenty minutes later, Gwen was carrying Debra Sue to the car.

Gwen was driving to the brace maker when she finally asked, "Debra Sue, why are you so rough on your leg brace? You are always breaking the straps on your leg brace. Now today, you broke the metal on your brace. What is going on?"

Debra Sue explained, "Mom, sometimes the teacher takes the class outside. I'm so slow when I walk down the stairs that I get left behind. So I jump down, skipping the last few steps on the stairs to keep up with the other students. Sometimes my strap breaks when I land on the floor. The teacher doesn't seem to care if I keep up with the class."

Gwen was furious and said, "After we get your brace fixed, I'm going to your school and have a talk with that teacher!"

Although Gwen kept her word and gave Debra Sue's teacher a piece of her mind, it didn't make much difference. The students still rushed by Debra Sue trying to squeeze in front of her before she reached the stairs. The students occasionally would still bump into Debra Sue and knock her down. And Debra Sue would continue to break the straps on her leg brace.

Gwen would continue to go to the brace maker for repairs. The brace maker felt sorry for Gwen because she was constantly having to pay for repairing Debra Sue's leg brace.

One day, the brace maker said, "Gwen, there is a place called the Houston Rehabilitation Center. If you take Debra Sue there, they will probably cover all of your expenses for Debra Sue's leg brace. Since I also work for them, you can't tell them I told you."

Gwen said, "Thank you for letting me know. I won't tell anyone you told me about them."

The next week, Gwen had an appointment for Debra Sue to meet with a doctor who specialized in polio patients at the Houston Rehabilitation Center. The doctor, the nurses, and the brace maker thoroughly evaluated Debra Sue.

They had Debra Sue walk around with her leg brace on in a private room. Debra Sue was relieved she didn't have to parade around in an arena with several other handicapped children like a bunch of cattle.

The doctor asked, "Debra Sue, can you walk without your leg brace on?"

Debra Sue replied, "Yes, if I keep my hand on my left knee to keep it from buckling."

The doctor said, "Show me how you walk without your leg brace."

Debra Sue took off her leg brace and walked around the room pressing her left hand against her left knee to keep it from buckling. After they thoroughly evaluated Debra Sue, the doctor sat down with Gwen.

The doctor said, "I have a team of doctors, and I believe we can perform two operations that may allow Debra Sue to walk without wearing a leg brace. We would need to perform surgery on Debra Sue's ankle to prevent the foot from dragging downward and surgery on her knee to allow it to lock automatically when she walks. We'll do both surgeries on the same day. She will need months of rehabilitation after the surgeries. Talk it over with your husband and let me know if you want to proceed."

Gwen said, "If two surgeries will allow Debra Sue to walk without a leg brace, I'm sure Sully will agree to the surgery. We will discuss it tonight and let you know if we want her to have the surgeries."

The doctor looked at the brace maker and said, "Now let's get Debra Sue fitted with a new leg brace that fits properly and has a prettier shoe."

The brace maker had Debra Sue sit on a flat table. He slipped a thick sheet of brown paper under Debra Sue's left leg. Then he took a black marker and drew an outline of her left leg. He took a tape measure and measured Debra Sue's thigh. He picked up a metal plate and measured Debra Sue's feet to determine what size shoe to attach to the brace.

The brace maker then opened a folder and showed Debra Sue a picture of the type of shoes she could pick from. Debra Sue picked out a pair of brown and white oxford shoes. The brace maker looked at Gwen and said, "The brace should be ready in two weeks. Make an appointment and we will see Debra Sue back in two weeks."

That evening at the dinner table, Gwen told Sully everything the doctor said about performing two surgeries that could allow Debra Sue to walk without a leg brace.

Sully said, "If the doctors feel the surgeries will allow Debra Sue to walk without a leg brace, then I think we should do it."

Stubborn Debra Sue shouted, "No! The doctors said that before! I have all these operations and go through all that pain, and I still can't walk without a brace! I don't want to go through all that pain again." Gwen reassuringly said, "These doctors are specialists. They seem confident the surgeries will be successful, and you will be able to walk without a leg brace. Don't you want to get rid of that brace and wear pretty shoes?"

That last statement allowed stubborn Debra Sue to change her mind and said, "I guess so. If I can wear pretty shoes, I guess it will be worth all of the pain."

Two weeks later, Gwen took Debra Sue to Houston Rehabilitation Center for her appointment. The brace maker walked into the room carrying a new leg brace with the shoe already attached and said, "Debra Sue, are you ready to try on your new brace?"

Debra Sue looked at her new leg brace with the brown and white oxford shoe that was attached to it and said, "At least the shoe is smaller, even though you still have to lace it up."

The brace maker said, "Well, let's try it on and see if it fits."

Debra Sue strapped on the leg brace and walked around. The brace maker asked, "How does that fit?"

Debra Sue replied, "It fits fine."

Although it was a new leg brace, she still thought the oxford shoe that was attached to it was ugly.

The brace maker said, "Okay. You can go then."

Gwen asked, "How much do I owe for the leg brace?"

The brace maker winked, smiled, and replied, "Nothing."

Debra Sue urgently said, "Okay, Mom, let's go."

Gwen and Debra walked quickly down the hallway snickering like they had just robbed a bank, and they were making their get-away. Once outside, Gwen said, "I feel like I'm stealing from them."

Debra Sue laughed and said, "Let's get to the car quickly."

Debra Sue walked as fast as she could with her new leg brace on. Gwen almost had to trot to keep up with her. They both had a good laugh once they climbed into the car. Gwen was very thankful that the brace maker had told her about the Houston Rehabilitation Center. She was also grateful that the brace maker also provided the shoes. It would be much more convenient for Gwen since she would no longer have to make an extra trip to the shoemaker.

Debra Sue was admitted to the hospital when she finished the seventh grade and was out for the summer. She was twelve years old when the doctor scheduled the surgery that would allow Debra Sue to lock her knee when walking and not have to wear that ugly leg brace with that ugly clodhopper shoe attached to it.

Debra Sue was admitted to the hospital on Monday morning, the day before her surgery. The surgery was scheduled for Tuesday at 1:00 p.m. The doctors were going to perform an ankle fusion to prevent her left foot from dragging downward. This would prevent her from tripping. Then the doctors would operate on her left knee to allow it to lock automatically as Debra Sue walked.

After being admitted into the hospital, a nurse took Gwen and Debra Sue to the recovery ward. The nurse looked at Gwen and said, "We are putting Debra Sue in the recovery ward for the night. This is where she will be taken after her surgery is completed tomorrow."

There were no other patients in the recovery ward when Debra Sue climbed into her bed. After Debra Sue was all settled in her bed, Gwen kissed her on the forehead and said, "I'm going now. You rest, and I'll see you in the morning before you go to surgery."

Debra Sue was scared and didn't want her mother to leave her all alone, but she put on a brave face, smiled, and said, "Okay. I love you, Mom."

Gwen said, "I love you to, sweetie," and left the ward.

At 5:00 p.m., a nurse walked into the recovery ward and asked, "Are you Debra Sue?"

Debra Sue replied, "Yes, ma'am."

The nurse looked at Debra Sue's wristband and frantically said, "Your surgery has been moved up from 1:00 p.m. in the afternoon to

7:00 a.m. in the morning. We can't get in touch with your mother to let her know. Do you have a phone number we can call?"

Debra Sue replied, "We just moved into a new house. I don't think the phone is hooked up yet."

The nurse said, "If your mom calls you, tell her your surgery has been moved up to 7:00 a.m."

Debra Sue was worried she wouldn't be able to get in touch with her mother but only said, "Yes, ma'am."

Although Debra Sue was only twelve years old, her young body had developed and matured early. Her body looked more like a sixteen-year-old than a twelve-year-old. All her girlfriends would often ask her if she stuffed her bra. Debra Sue would blush and embarrassingly say, "No!"

Once when Debra Sue was eleven, while having a sleepover with her girlfriends, there was a bully in the group. The bully talked two other girls into holding Debra Sue down on the bed so she could prove Debra Sue was stuffing her bra. After lifting up her blouse, they never ask Debra Sue if she stuffed her bra again.

So with her body maturing at a young age, being left all alone in the hospital, and the stress she was under from facing a surgery all alone, it was no wonder and very unfortunate that Debra Sue would start her menstrual period that evening.

Now Debra Sue was an extremely shy girl, and she was not about to ask a nurse for a Kotex. Debra Sue thought, *Why couldn't Mom stay here with me. Doesn't she know I'm scared to death to have this surgery? And now I'm on my period, and I'm all alone. I wish she was here so she could get me a Kotex.*

The trauma became too much for Debra Sue to bear, and she broke down and started to cry. When there were no more tears to shed, stubborn Debra Sue knew she would have to take care of herself.

She placed her hand on her left knee and carefully walked to the bathroom. She cleaned her underwear with a paper towel. Then she wrapped several handfuls of toilet paper and placed it inside her underwear.

She walked cautiously back to her bed and climbed in. She hoped the doctors wouldn't notice her stained underwear when she had her surgery tomorrow. Debra Sue felt all alone in the empty recovery ward, and she started sobbing.

At 8:00 p.m., a young male intern walked into the recovery ward. He noticed the ward was empty except for Debra Sue. The male intern said, "I need to take your vital statistics."

He took Debra Sue's temperature, blood pressure and listened to her heartbeat. Then all of a sudden, he reached down and opened the front of Debra Sue's underwear and took a peek. With quick cat-like response, Debra Sue slapped his hand away and screamed, "Stop it!" Debra Sue was so angry and humiliated because she had a wad of toilet paper tucked in her underwear.

The male intern stammered, "I'm...I'm...I'm so sorry," and quickly left the room.

Debra Sue thought, *Why isn't my mother here with me,* and started to cry. She cried herself to sleep. She had a restless and fitful night, tossing and turning all night long.

At 5:30 a.m., Debra Sue put her hand on her knee and hobbled to the restroom. She replaced her toilet paper in her underwear with a new wad of toilet paper. Debra Sue thought, *I wish Mom was here so she could get me a Kotex before my surgery.*

At 6:00 a.m., a female nurse came into the room and said, "You have to take a sponge bath so you will be clean for surgery."

She pulled up a chair next to the bed and handed a tub of warm water, soap, and washcloth to Debra Sue. Debra Sue shyly took off her gown while the nurse was watching her.

Debra Sue wanted to shout, *What are you staring at you, nosy nurse?*

But Debra Sue quietly and discretely pulled off her underwear with the toilet paper rolled up inside them. She hid the rolled-up underwear inside her gown. She was hoping the nurse gawking at her didn't see the toilet paper.

After Debra Sue sponged bath herself, she put back on her stained underwear with the toilet paper still inside. She then put on her hospital gown. The nurse took the tub of water and washcloth and left the room.

At 6:30 a.m., a nurse walked into recovery ward and asked, "Did you get in touch with your mother?"

Debra Sue replied, "No, ma'am."

The nurse said, "I'm going to wheel you to the operating room now."

Debra Sue asked, "You're not going to wait for my mother?"

The nurse replied, "No, honey. We have to go now. The doctors are waiting."

Debra Sue thought, *This is so embarrassing. I sure hope the doctors don't see my wad of toilet paper in my underwear.*

Since the nurses could not get in touch with Gwen, Debra Sue was all by herself when the nurses wheeled her to the operating room at 6:45 a.m. Debra Sue couldn't fight back the tears anymore, and the tears started streaming down her cheeks. A nurse squeezed her hand and reassuring said, "Everything is going to be okay, darling."

After the surgery, Debra Sue awoke in the recovery room. Gwen eyes were red and swollen from crying as she hovered over Debra Sue and said, "I'm so sorry I wasn't here before you went into surgery."

Debra Sue made an excuse for her mother and said, "That's okay, Mom. They moved up the surgery, and they didn't have your phone number. I told them we just moved into a new house, and I didn't think the phone was hooked up yet."

Debra Sue looked down and saw a bloody cast on her left leg that ran from her toes to above her knee. There were two long steel rods running the length of the cast on both sides.

There was a short bar running into the cast, through the ankle-bone and then out of the cast that connected to the lower part of the long steel bar. There was another short bar running into the cast, through the leg bone just below the knee and out of the cast that connected to the top part of the long bar.

Then Debra Sue remembered she was on her period. She hoped the doctors didn't see her wad of toilet paper in her underwear. She opened her gown and noticed she was wearing a Kotex and a Kotex belt. Debra Sue thought, *So much for them not noticing my wad of toilet paper in my underwear. I didn't know they made a Kotex belt to hold up a Kotex. I'm going to be so embarrassed when the doctors walk in.*

Debra Sue remembered what the male intern did and said, "Mom, last night a male intern took my blood pressure, temperature, and listened to my heartbeat. Then he pulled open my underwear and took a peek. You need to tell someone about that pervert."

Now Gwen was naive when it came to doctors and said, "Honey, he is a doctor, and doctors sometimes have to examine your privates." Debra Sue was irritated that her mom was so naive and said, "The doctors were operating on my leg, Mom. Not on my privates. If I wasn't on my period, he probably would have molested me."

Gwen chuckled and said, "You're overreacting, sweetie. He is a doctor. He wouldn't do that."

Debra Sue did not think it was funny and sternly said, "What the doctor did was wrong, and he should be reported!"

Gwen gave Debra Sue a hug and repeated, "You're overreacting, sweetie, but I will tell the head doctor."

Debra Sue said, "Thank you, Mom." But knew she would not be able to convince her mother that a doctor might do something wrong or illegal.

Debra Sue moaned from the pain and started crying. Gwen caressed Debra Sue's forehead and choked back the tears and said, "There is no way I will be scratching your leg with a coat hanger this time."

Debra Sue said, "That's okay. My leg hurts so much I don't want anyone to touch it."

The doctor walked into the room and sat next to Gwen and said, "I inserted several screws in the ankle to fuse the ankle. That will keep the ankle from dropping. I inserted two steel rods to hold the ankle up while the bones fuse together. However, Debra Sue lost a lot of blood during the surgery on her ankle, and we were unable to perform the operation on her knee. That is why her cast is blood stained. We will perform the knee surgery after her ankle heals. I will check in on her later," and left the room.

The operation on Debra Sue's ankle turned out to be another very painful one. Debra Sue would often cry out during the night because of the excruciating pain. The pain medication didn't seem to help much.

Three days later, Debra Sue was moved into a semiprivate room. But she had the whole room to herself. The nurses probably put Debra Sue into an unoccupied semiprivate room because they didn't want Debra Sue waking a patient in the next bed when she cried out in pain during the middle of the night.

Two weeks later, a nurse brought in a wheelchair that had a straight board sticking out on the left side. The nurse said, "Debra Sue, it's time for you to get up and move around so you can go home. What do you think about that?"

Debra Sue said, "My ankle still hurts all the time."

The nurse said, "That's why you need to get up and move around so your ankle will heal."

Debra Sue said, "Okay. I want to go home."

The nurse kept Debra Sue's left leg elevated as she helped Debra Sue get into the wheelchair. Then the nurse gently laid her cast with the bars protruding out onto the board that was attached to the wheelchair. The nurse asked Debra Sue, "Can you wheel yourself into the hallway and back to your room?"

Stubborn Debra Sue said, "I sure can."

Debra Sue grabbed a hold of her wheels and started pushing herself out into the hallway. She was glad to finally be out of her room. She wheeled herself up and down the hallways until the pain became too intense, and then she wheeled herself back to her room.

For the next week, stubborn Debra Sue rolled herself up and down the hallways in spite of the pain she had to endure. After three weeks of being in the hospital, it was finally time for Debra Sue to go home. After Gwen checked Debra Sue out of the hospital, a nurse pushed Debra Sue in her wheelchair to the hospital exit doors.

While Gwen was getting the car, the nurse retrieved a pair of crutches and handed them to Debra Sue. The nurse said, "You will need these crutches to help you walk."

Gwen parked the car by the hospital exit doors and ran around the car and opened the passenger front door and said, "Okay, honey. Let's go home."

Debra Sue grabbed the crutches and stood up for the first time in seven weeks. The pain was excruciating as the blood rushed down to her left ankle and immediately started throbbing. It felt like a sledgehammer hitting her ankle each time the ankle throbbed. Tears started running down her cheeks as Debra Sue hobbled to the car.

On the way home, Gwen said, "We're going to stop at a restaurant and get something to eat. That will take your mind off of your pain. I'll give you a pain pill in the restaurant."

They stopped off at a burger restaurant. Debra Sue was in pain and didn't feel like eating, but she climbed out of the car and hobbled into the restaurant.

She was in agony with each step she took. When they finally finished eating, Debra Sue hobbled back to the car. The pain pill didn't seem to help much as they drove home.

Debra Sue climbed into her bed and was so thankful she could finally rest her leg in an up position to ease the throbbing pain. The ankle surgery proved to be very painful for Debra Sue. She had many sleepless nights because the pain would often awaken her. It was difficult for her to walk because of the pain.

After being home for five weeks, it was time to see the doctor. Debra Sue was glad it was time to visit the doctor. She was getting bored being stuck in the house every day.

The doctor informed Gwen that it was time to remove Debra Sue's cast and perform the knee-lock surgery. The doctor told Gwen to admit Debra Sue into the hospital next week on Monday. They would remove the cast on Monday and then perform the surgery on Tuesday.

Gwen and Debra Sue had just returned home from visiting with the doctor. The doctor said they would take off the cast next week. Debra Sue was hobbling from the car to the front door when she saw a cockroach. She shuddered with disgust.

A couple days later, Debra Sue's ankle was feeling like something was crawling all over it, and it gave her an eerie feeling. When Gwen came into her room, Debra Sue said, "Mom, it feels like roaches are crawling on my ankle."

Gwen said, "That's ridiculous. There's no roaches crawling around on your ankle."

Debra Sue said, "I saw a cockroach the other day when we came home from the doctor. I think it crawled into my cast and had babies."

Gwen reassuringly said, "No cockroach climbed into your cast and had babies. It is just itching because your ankle is healing. The doctor said they are going to take off the cast on Monday. You only have to wear that cast a few more days."

Nine weeks after Debra Sue's ankle surgery, the doctors admitted Debra Sue back into the hospital. Just like last time, the nurse took Debra Sue to the recovery ward and pointed to a bed and said, "This is your bed, Debra Sue. This is where you will be tomorrow after your operation. Your mother can visit you here in the morning before you go into surgery."

Gwen made sure Debra Sue was comfortable in her room before leaving. The hospital was strict when enforcing the visiting hours. Gwen leaned over and gave Debra Sue a kiss on the forehead and said, "I'll see you in the morning before you go into surgery."

Debra Sue, said, "Okay. I love you, Mom."

At 3:00 p.m., a nurse walked into the recovery ward pushing an empty wheelchair. She walked over to Debra Sue's bed and asked, "Are you Debra Sue?"

Debra Sue replied, "Yes, ma'am."

The nurse looked at Debra Sue's wristband and said, "I'm taking you to the cast room so they can remove the cast on your leg."

Debra Sue said, "About time. My ankle itches so bad. I can't wait to scratch it."

The nurse pushed Debra Sue to the cast room and said, "The intern that is going to remove the cast and steel rods should be here any minute now."

About five minutes later, an intern entered the cast room. Debra Sue felt her body grow tense when she recognized the intern. It was the same pervert intern that tried to peek down her panties when she had her last operation.

The intern was uncomfortable also, and he refused to look her in the eyes when he stammered, "I'm…I'm going to remove your cast and the steel rods in your leg and ankle."

The intern was silent as he removed the nuts and bolts attached to the short and long bars. He sawed through the cast, and then he pried open the top part of the cast. He removed the bar that ran through Debra Sue's leg just below her knee. It came out without too much difficulty. The nurse was chatting and laughing as she assisted the intern.

Then the intern pried open the cast by the ankle. All of a sudden, the nurse stopped chatting and laughing and became very silent and serious. The intern was mortified and turned pale after seeing Debra Sue's ankle and immediately said, "You need to lie down. I don't want you to see this."

Debra Sue asked, "Why? What's wrong?"

The intern ignored Debra Sue's question as he pried off the cast. He tried to pull out the steel rod from Debra Sue's ankle. It was stuck in all that rotting meat.

The intern told the nurse to push on the steel rod while he pulled on it. The nurse pushed, and the intern pulled, and they still couldn't remove the steel rod. The intern finally retrieved a hammer and started to pound on the steel rod.

The nurse asked Debra Sue, "Are you in a lot of pain, honey."

Debra Sue gritted her teeth and said, "I'm okay."

After pounding on the steel rod with several blows, the rod finally broke loose, and they were able to remove the rod from Debra Sue's ankle. When the steel rod was removed, the nurse called the doctor.

The doctor walked in and took one look at Debra Sue's ankle and immediately ordered, "Get her a private room and have it sterilized right now! I want her in isolation!"

Stubborn Debra Sue knew something was wrong when the doctor used that tone of voice and tried to sit up and take a look at her ankle. The doctor grabbed Debra Sue on the shoulders and gently lay her back down and said, "You need to rest, sweetheart."

The doctor started cleaning the wound and removing the dead flesh. The doctor realized the infection was very serious, and he contemplated amputating the foot above the ankle to prevent gangrene from setting in. The doctor commented to himself, "I sure hope we can get this infection under control."

The doctor cleaned the wound and gently placed a piece of gauze over the ankle. He ordered the nurse to hook up an IV and put Debra Sue on a megadose of antibiotics. The doctor squeezed Debra Sue's hand and said, "You're a tough young lady. I'll have the hospital notify your parents so they can come visit you."

Debra Sue asked, "Am I still having my surgery tomorrow?"

The doctor replied, "Heavens no. You won't be having that operation until your ankle is healed."

Stubborn Debra Sue couldn't believe they weren't going to operate on her knee in the morning and again asked, "You're not going to operate on my knee tomorrow?"

The doctor curtly said, "No," and left the room.

Debra Sue was upset she wasn't having the operation in the morning and started to cry. The nurse asked, "Are you in pain, honey?"

Debra Sue replied, "A little."

The nurse said, "I'm going to wheel you to the recovery ward until your room is sterilized."

The nurse pushed Debra Sue to the recovery ward and helped her into a vacant bed. Then the nurse hooked Debra Sue up to an IV containing the megadose of antibiotics so that it could start battling her infection.

As Debra Sue was waiting for her private room to be sanitized, her ankle started throbbing, and the pain became intense from where the intern was pounding on the steel rod with a hammer. Debra Sue couldn't take the pain anymore and asked a nurse passing by, "Can I have something for pain?"

The passing by nurse said, "Sure. I'll get you a popsicle."

Stubborn Debra Sue yelled, "A popsicle!"

The passing by nurse said, "Yes, a popsicle."

About two hours later, Debra Sue was wheeled to her sanitized private room. The nurse who passed by never did bring Debra Sue a popsicle to ease her pain. Debra Sue's sanitized private room was an isolation room.

No one would be allowed to enter the room unless they were wearing a gown, mask, gloves, surgeon's cap, and covers over their shoes. Every hour on the hour, a nurse would walk into the room wearing a gown, mask, glove, and surgeon's cap.

The nurse would carefully clean the wound with hydrogen peroxide and put medication on it. Then they would lightly place a new gauze over the wound. That was how serious Debra Sue's infection was.

At 8:00 p.m., Gwen walked into Debra Sue's private room. She was wearing a gown, mask, gloves, cap over her hair, and slippers over her shoes. Debra Sue could tell her mother had been crying. I guess she realized how serious the infection was when she was asked to put on all this protective gear.

Gwen leaned over and gave Debra Sue a kiss on her forehead through her face mask and asked, "How are you feeling? Are you in pain?"

Debra Sue replied, "I'm okay, Mom."

Gwen asked, "Can I see your ankle?"

Debra Sue said, "No! It's gross-looking!"

Gwen said, "Come on. Let me take a look."

Debra Sue said, "It's going to make you sick."

Gwen gently lifted the gauze off the ankle. Gwen was silent and looked a little pale after gazing at the wound. She gently laid the gauze over the wound and sat down in the chair. She wiped the tears that started to run down her cheeks and said, "Everything is going to be okay."

The next morning, the doctor told Gwen and Sully that he would be unable to perform the knee surgery due to Debra Sue's infection. He let Gwen and Sully know that he might have to amputate her foot above the ankle if they couldn't get the infection under control quickly. Gwen broke down and cried. Sully put his arm around Gwen and reassured her.

Sully said, "Debra Sue is a stubborn girl. She will beat this infection, she will have the knee operation, and she will walk without a leg brace. She is my strong soldier girl."

Every day, Gwen would put on a hospital gown, mask, gloves, and surgeon's cap and go sit by her brave little girl. After four weeks in isolation, the infection was under control, and Debra Sue was moved to a semiprivate room. Debra Sue spent four more weeks in a semiprivate room.

After being in the hospital for two months, the doctor was finally ready to schedule Debra Sue for her knee operation. The ankle surgery proved to be a very long and painful surgery for Debra Sue. And now she was facing yet another surgery. How much more would stubborn Debra Sue have to endure?

Debra Older

*Chapter 15*

## THE LOCK-KNEE SURGERY

DEBRA SUE HAD BEEN in the hospital for two full months. And now she was going to be staying in the hospital for another few weeks. The nasty infection had been eliminated, and Debra Sue's ankle had finally healed. The doctor was now ready to perform the lock-knee surgery on Debra Sue's left knee.

The morning of Debra Sue's surgery, Gwen kissed Debra Sue on her forehead and said, "I love you, sweetie."

Debra Sue groggily said, "I love you, Mom."

After the operation was completed, Debra Sue was moved to the recovery ward. The doctor walked in and sat down next to Gwen and said, "The operation on her knee went as planned. She will be in the cast for six weeks. After we remove the cast, it will take months of physical therapy to get the knee to lock on its own and allow her to walk without a leg brace."

Debra Sue had been awake for about five minutes and groggily asked, "I won't have to wear that ugly clodhopper shoe anymore?"

The doctor chuckled and replied, "If everything goes to plan, then yes. But it will take months of hard work and physical therapy. Can you do that for me?"

Stubborn Debra Sue replied, "Yes, sir. I will do anything not to have to wear that ugly clodhopper shoe." Debra Sue looked down at her left leg and saw a cast running from her foot to her thigh. Debra Sue thought, *I hope I don't get another infection.*

Debra Sue asked the doctor, "Why is my leg bent? Shouldn't it be straight so my knee can lock?"

The doctor replied, "The knee has to be slightly bent so it can heal properly. After the cast is removed, then you will begin straightening out the leg. This will take months of physical therapy before the knee starts to lock on its own. Can you do months of physical therapy for me?"

Debra Sue replied, "I sure can."

After three days of bed rest, the nurse came into the ward and said, "We're going to move your bed to a semiprivate room." The nurses unlocked the wheels and pushed Debra Sue to a semiprivate room.

It was the same room she stayed in when she was in isolation because of her infection. Debra Sue thought, *Not this room again. At least I'm by myself.*

The next morning, a nurse walked in and said, "Debra Sue, it's time for you to get out of bed and start your physical therapy."

Stubborn Debra Sue said, "Okay. I'm ready to get out of this hospital."

Debra Sue sat up and turned sideways, letting her left leg dangle over the edge of the bed. The throbbing started immediately, and this surgery proved to be just as painful as all the other surgeries. Debra Sue asked, "Can I have something for pain?"

The nurse replied, "After you walk to the restroom and back to your bed."

The nurse handed Debra Sue a pair of crutches, helped her out of the bed, and steadied her on her feet. Debra Sue took her first step since the surgery and moaned out in pain. Then she took her next step, then another and another. She walked to the restroom and was thankful she no longer needed a bed pan.

After returning to her bed, Debra Sue asked the nurse, "May I have something for pain now?"

The nurse said, "Yes," and left the ward.

Debra Sue's knee was throbbing in pain with each pulse her heartbeat made. The nurse made Debra Sue suffer in pain for twenty minutes before returning to the ward with her pain medication.

Debra Sue wanted to scream, *About time, you mean old witch*, but only said, "Thank you."

The next few days, Debra Sue grimaced from the pain, as she walked up and down the hall with her crutches. One day, Debra Sue had walked up and down the hall and had just returned to her bed, when two nurses walked into her room. There were two very seductive magazines lying on top of the covers.

Both nurses noticed the seductive magazines on the bed. One gasped, "Lordy, mercy!" while the other one gasped, "Oh my goodness! Does your mother know you have these types of magazines?"

Debra Sue blushed and replied, "Yes. She is the one who brought them to me."

The nurses shook their heads in disgust, and one nurse said, "Goodness, gracious," and they left the room.

During the next three weeks, the nurses became much friendlier with Debra Sue. They would often come into her room and sit down to watch TV or to read her seductive magazines. Even the nurses that gasped, "Lordy, mercy," and "Oh my goodness," would read the seductive magazines.

As Debra Sue watched the nurses reading the seductive magazines, she thought, *For someone who disapproves of my seductive magazines, they sure don't have a problem with reading them.*

Finally, three weeks after her surgery, the doctors released Debra Sue from the hospital. Debra Sue was finally going home after being in the hospital for over four months.

Debra Sue remembered the last time when her mother stopped at a restaurant on the way home from the hospital and how painful it was to hobble into the restaurant. Debra Sue said, "Please, don't stop at a restaurant on the way home. I'm not hungry."

Gwen said, "Okay, sweetie."

Gwen drove straight home. When Debra Sue walked into the house, there was a banner strung in the living room saying, "Happy Birthday." Debra Sue had been in so much pain, she had forgotten that it was her birthday. All she wanted to do was go lie down and rest.

But stubborn Debra Sue put on a fake smile when the family sang "Happy Birthday" to her. She gave everyone a hug and then opened her presents. One present was a Polaroid camera. The type of camera that would print out the picture seconds after you snapped it. She took a picture of the family. Then Gwen took the camera and said, "Smile, Debra Sue."

Debra Sue put on another fake smile, and Gwen snapped a picture of Debra Sue and her birthday cake.

Debra Sue asked her mother, "Can I have something for pain?"

Gwen said, "Of course you can," and gave Debra Sue a pain pill.

Debra Sue was relieved that she didn't have to wait twenty minutes before getting something to relieve her pain. It was wonderful to finally be back home. Debra Sue was tired, and her knee was aching. Debra Sue asked, "Mom, can I sleep on the couch? I don't want Terry bumping into my leg during the night."

Gwen said, "You sure can, sweetie. Let me go get you some blankets." Gwen went to her bedroom and came back with a pillow, sheet, and blanket. Gwen tucked the sheet into the couch and patted the pillow at the end of the couch.

After a long and painful day, Debra Sue was finally able to lie down on the couch and rest. Debra Sue said, "Thanks, Mom." The days past, and Debra Sue was able to be more mobile with less pain. The knee itched from time to time, and Debra Sue would take the clothes hanger that she straightened and maneuver it inside the cast to scratch her leg. She was hoping her knee wasn't infected like her ankle had been, but that didn't stop Debra Sue from scratching her leg with the clothes hanger anyway.

Finally, after six weeks, it was time for the doctors to remove Debra Sue's cast. Gwen took Debra Sue to the hospital. At the hospital, the nurse escorted them to the cast room. The intern removed the cast. This time there was no infection.

The doctor came in and examined Debra Sue's knee and said, "The knee looks great. Are you ready to start the long road of physical therapy?"

Debra Sue replied, "Yes, sir."

The doctor smiled and said, "That's good to hear. I'll see you back in one month after you have completed some physical therapy."

The doctor left the room, and an intern escorted Gwen and Debra Sue to the physical therapy room. There was a nurse and a young female physical therapist waiting for Debra Sue.

The physical therapist said, "Debra Sue, I want you to go over to the two handlebars on either side of the mat. I want you to use the handlebars instead of your crutches to walk from one end to the other."

The physical therapist observed Debra Sue as she walked to the end of the handlebars, turned around, and walked back to the other end of the handlebars.

The young therapist looked at Gwen and said, "There's nothing we can do. That knee will never lock on its own. She will never be able to walk without a leg brace. My recommendation is that Debra Sue be fitted for a leg brace immediately."

Debra Sue became very distraught. With tears streaming down her face, she asked the young therapist, "You're not going to have me do physical therapy?"

The young therapist replied, "There's nothing we can do. The knee will never lock on its own. The only way you will be able to walk is with a leg brace."

On the drive home, Debra Sue was heartbroken and was sobbing. Gwen tried to lift Debra Sue's spirit and said, "Honey, a leg brace isn't so bad. You're an old pro at getting around in a leg brace."

Stubborn Debra Sue angrily said, "I'm not going back to wearing a leg brace ever again! If it isn't so bad, then you can wear the leg brace! How's that!"

Gwen and Debra Sue remained silent the rest of the ride home. Stubborn Debra Sue had made up her mind that she would never wear a leg brace again. Every day, and throughout the day, for thirty days straight, Debra Sue would place her foot on a pillow and then pressed down hard on her knee so her leg would be extended straight out. Sometimes it was so painful, it would bring tears to her eyes.

Debra Sue wanted to prove that physical therapist was a liar when she stated the knee would never lock on its own. Debra Sue started to practice walking without placing her hand above her knee. She closed her eyes and pretended her hand was on her left knee. Then with her mind, she willed her knee to lock on its own.

Debra Sue took a step, making sure her toes landed on the floor before her heel did. The knee locked on its own. Debra Sue took another step, then another, and on the third step, her heel landed on the floor before her toes did. Her left knee buckled, and she landed hard on the floor, bruising her right knee.

Debra Sue refused to let that misstep stop her. She stood up and started all over again. After walking about ten steps, her knee buckled again, and she hit the floor hard, this time skinning her bruised knee. Stubborn Debra Sue grimaced with pain as she stood up. She placed her hand above her knee as she walked over to the light switch. The knee locked easily when Debra Sue placed just a little pressure above her knee with her hand. But she was going to prove that the physical therapist was a liar.

Debra Sue turned off the light so she could concentrate. With her mind, Debra Sue willed her knee to lock on its own. She made sure her toes landed on the floor before her heel, and she walked up and down the length of her bedroom. Stubborn Debra Sue was walking without pressing her hand above her knee.

Debra Sue sat down on her bed with a big grin on her face. She couldn't wait until she showed the doctor that she could walk without a brace. Then the pain in her right knee started to take over, and Debra Sue lay down on the bed and rested.

A month later, Gwen took Debra Sue to the doctor. They were waiting in the examining room when the doctor, an intern, and the young physical therapist walked into the room. The doctor read Debra Sue's chart that was hanging on the door.

The doctor explained to the intern that he performed a lock-knee type of surgery. That it would keep Debra Sue's leg from buckling, and it would allow her to walk without a leg brace.

Then the doctor examined Debra Sue's knee. He had Debra Sue extend her left leg on the table and measured her knee as it was extended. The doctor said, "Everything is progressing like it should." The doctor read the physical therapist notes and recommendation stating that the patient's knee would not lock and would require a leg brace. The doctor was infuriated and yelled at the therapist, "You're making that statement after seeing the patient walk on your first session! You don't know what you are talking about! Debra Sue has been immobilized for six months! Of course, she won't be able to straighten her leg for quite some time! That knee will lock! But it is going to take months of physical therapy! Debra Sue is willing to do the physical therapy! Aren't you, Debra Sue?"

Debra Sue smiled and said, "I sure am. I've been extending my leg and pushing down on the knee every day. That therapist only let me walk up and down the handlebars once. Then she said my knee would never lock, and I would have to wear a leg brace."

The doctor said, "That therapist doesn't know what she is talking about. Can you try walking up and down the room without your crutches?"

Debra Sue asked, "Can I take off my shoes? I've been practicing walking barefoot."

The doctor said, "You sure can."

Debra Sue took off her shoes and socks and laid them on the table. She swung her legs over the edge of the table. Whenever Debra Sue pulled herself on or off a table, she would hook her right foot under her left ankle and carry the left leg on or off the table. Debra Sue was so subtle when she did this maneuver, most doctors didn't even notice. Stubborn Debra Sue wanted to look as normal as possible.

Debra Sue stood up and pressed her left hand above her left knee and took a step. The knee had locked and not buckled. She walked to the end of the room, turned around, and walked back toward the doctor. Debra Sue took her hand away from her knee as she made the last few steps to the doctor. As long as she made sure that her toes hit the floor before her heel, she was able to lock her knee and keep it from buckling.

The doctor was ecstatic and said, "I knew the knee-lock surgery was successful. You can get back onto the table, Debra Sue."

Debra Sue pulled herself onto the table. She hooked her right foot behind her left ankle and carried her left foot onto the table with her right leg. The doctor was amazed at what Debra Sue just did and asked the intern, "Did you notice how she got onto the table?"

The intern replied, "She just pulled herself up onto the table."

The doctor said, "She has little muscle control in her left leg. She hooked her right foot behind her left ankle and carried the left leg up onto the table with her right leg. She does it so subtly, I bet most physicians don't even notice. They probably think she has muscles in both legs." The doctor instructed Debra Sue to extend her left leg on the table. He placed his hand on her left knee and pressed down and said, "Debra Sue, I need you to continue extending your left leg and pressing down on your knee just like you have been doing at home. Can you do that every day?"

Debra Sue replied, "Yes, sir. Will I be going to physical therapy?"

The doctor sternly said, "No! The physical therapist doesn't know what she is doing! I don't want you going back to her. You know what to do. Keep pressing down on your knee every day, several times during the day. Your leg will eventually extend to the point where the knee will lock on its own. I'll see you in six weeks."

The doctor, the intern, and the physical therapist left the examination room. Debra Sue smiled as she thought, *I'm glad the doctor chewed out that physical therapist. I'll never go back to wearing a leg brace again.*

Debra Sue did exactly what the doctor wanted her to do. She would extend her leg and press down hard on her knee to get it to straighten out. Sometimes she would press down so hard it would bring tears to her eyes.

Stubborn Debra Sue never relented on doing her physical therapy. After eighteen months of constant physical therapy, Debra Sue was finally able to put her crutches in the closet. She was ecstatic that she no longer required crutches to walk.

Debra Sue had to make sure her toes would land on the floor before her heel did when she was walking. Therefore, she had to wear flat-soled shoes because shoes with a heel would make her knee buckle and cause her to fall down.

Although Debra Sue was disappointed that she could not wear high heel shoes, she was thankful she no longer required a leg brace. The surgeries were a success. Debra Sue no longer had to use crutches, wear a leg brace, or wear ugly shoes.

Debra Sue went on to graduate high school and then married her high school sweetheart. Debra Sue then had a baby girl. Because of her polio, Debra Sue had to have a cesarean section on her first-born. The doctors recommended Debra Sue not to have any more children because of her polio. The doctors said raising a child would be too exhausting for someone having polio. Plus, she would have to have another cesarean section which would be too dangerous for her.

Six years later, stubborn Debra Sue gave birth by cesarean section to a baby boy. Debra Sue refused to let her handicap stop her from accomplishing her goals. Debra Sue raised a family, went to college, and made a career as a computer programmer. She made computer programs for several companies that included a major airline company, the postal service, the Tip Top Janitorial Services, and a Baptist church.

Stubborn Debra Sue demonstrated all through her childhood that *where there is a will, there is a way.*

James and Gwen

James and Debra

Debra and Jeff

Debra holding block

'The photo of Debra Sue holding the block was the last photo taken, before she was afflicted with polio. It brings tears to my eyes seeing this 'cutie, matudie' and knowing the pain and suffering this little girl would have to endure. Stubborn Debra Sue is and always will be my hero.—Jeffery Tracey Sr.

## *About the Author*

JEFFERY TRACEY SR. WAS born April 2, 1952, in Mt. Vernon, Ohio. His family separated when he was two, reunited when he was six, and separated again when he was eleven. After the last separation, Jeffery was sent to a foster home for four years.

He kept a positive attitude and graduated from South Houston High School in 1970. He married his wife, Debra, and then started his career in the US Postal Service. He was a letter carrier and then was promoted to supervisor, then manager. In 2000, he was acting postmaster in Livingston, Texas.

He and his wife currently reside in Pearland, Texas, where they have been residents for twenty-six years. He has a daughter, son, and six grandchildren. After raising a family and dedicating his life to the US Postal Service, he started working on his passion of writing short stories.

His first book, *A Family Reunited,* released by Page Publishing Inc., is a collection of true short stories about a young boy reunited with an older brother, then father, and finally, two more older brothers. It then tells about the boy's wild adventures living on a farm in the Midwest in the early sixties.

His second book, *A Family Torn Apart,* released by Page Publishing Inc., is a heart-wrenching true story about an eleven-year-old boy who sees his family being torn apart because of alcoholism, abuse, abandonment, and poverty.

His third book, *Brainwashed by Foster Parents,* was released by Page Publishing Inc. It is a true story of a young boy who was manipulated, coerced, and brainwashed by his foster parents.

His fourth book, *Stubborn Debra Sue,* was recently released by Page Publishing Inc. It is an inspirational story based on true events about a little handicapped girl who never gave up. It tells about the agony the little girl endured with her many operations. It tells how the little girl refused to let her handicap keep her from doing what other kids her age were doing. She gives true meaning to the phrase "Where there is a will, there is a way."